Feed Your Business

Secrets from a Google Insider: Outrank 90% of Your Google Shopping Competitors Before Spending a Dime

Kevin J. Wetherby

Mind Candy Publishing

FEED YOUR BUSINESS

Copyright © 2022 by Kevin J. Wetherby

All rights reserved.

No portion of this book may be reproduced in any form without written permission from the publisher or author, except as permitted by U.S. copyright law.

Book cover designed by Eddie Roseboom

To my wife Mary who inspires me every day. Thank you for believing in me.

Contents

Foreword	1
1. Introduction	3
2. Google Merchant Center	7
3. GMC Account Setting	11
4. GMC Account Tools	22
5. GMC Products Tab	46
6. Product Feed Specifications and Formatting	53
7. Methods to Create a Product Feed	66
8. Shopify's Google Channel App	77
9. Submitting Your Feed	82
10. Product Feed Optimization	88
11. Troubleshooting Common Product Feed Problems	100
12. Google Merchant Center Feed Rules	112
13. Parting Thoughts	120
Acknowledgments	123
About the Author	124

Foreword

The marketing world is full of thin and theoretical advice that diverts your attention from the prize.

Thankfully, inside this book you have a hands-on approach of not just setting up, but actually optimising your shopping feed.

And it is packed with real-life examples so you can start taking action *immediately*.

If you have run Google Shopping before, you will know that keyword targeting does not exist as a feature.

Yes, you can add negative keywords against the search terms that appear for products, but you cannot explicitly control that target.

With the introduction of Smart Shopping and now Performance Max, those controls (or lack of) have become even more restricted. That is where the power of feed optimisation comes in.

With the aforementioned Performance Max (and its predecessor Smart Shopping) limiting control even further, your shopping feed has to do a lot of the heavy lifting.

In fact, your shopping feed is so critical – it can be the difference between a positive return on ad spend, or falling flat and burning money. In that respect, Shopping feed optimisation is the 80/20 of shopping ads.

Sure - you can fiddle with features inside Google Ads. You can tweak and fettle your campaigns. But if your feed is suboptimal, then you are limiting your performance.

That is where Kevin's book comes in to play.

Kevin has extensive experience in this space – including a good chunk of it at Google – and has laboured over giving you every facet required to setup, optimise and scale your shopping ads via 'proper' feed management.

It is full of examples and specific directions that will ensure you take your feed from 'okay' to really honed. Which is precisely what you need to maximise your Ad returns.

Like Kevin, I've been around Google Advertising for well over a decade now. I have read enough books to know when to relegate them to the dusty shelf and when to keep them close to my side – "Feed Your Business" is very much in the latter category. It will adorn my desk for many months to come.

I might even have to steal a few ideas for myself...

Thank you to Kevin for inviting me to write this foreword. I hope you enjoy the book; I know I did.

Ed Leake
www.edleake.com

Chapter One

Introduction

The "Aha" Moment

About 15 years ago, when I first started working with product data feeds, I was onboarding a large Fortune 500 company that sold shoes. In optimizing the feed, I was shocked at how sparse the titles were. Here I was, looking at the title "Princess" and there was no other data attached to it. That is, there was no other data or information in the title that told you what the product was.

If you were on the product page of this retailer's website, it would be obvious what the product was. You would see the brand name not far from the title. The title still only had "Princess" in it, but combined with the image next to it and the description below it, you had a pretty good idea that this was a little girl's sneaker.

The problem is when you separate the data from the website, each field stands on its own. From a search standpoint, with the title only being "Princess," it would not show up for relevant search terms. You certainly would not want it to appear in the search results when someone searches for an actual princess from Disney or a storybook character.

This was that "aha" moment. I realized that here is a Fortune 500 company with significant money and resources behind them, and the data that was being sent to me was insufficient! I knew at that moment that this problem was far-reaching. Could the average shop owner have better data? Most likely they would not. There was a very real need for feed optimization. This led me to another profound realization: With a little bit of information and some effort, the average shop owner could surpass these large corporate eCommerce stores by following best practices and improving their data!

Getting back to my story. The fix to the title issue was combining several attributes found in the feed. By adding the brand name ("Acme"—not the real brand) and then the gender (Girls), followed by the title (Princess), and finally appending the product type (Sneaker) we came up with the following: Acme Girls Princess Sneaker. From a search engine optimization (SEO) standpoint this was a much better title and would be included in many searches. And more importantly, the product probably would not show up for non-relevant searches such as "princess." We could take this one step further and add size (6) and our final optimized title would be: Acme Girls Princess Sneaker Size 6. Beautiful!

Later in the book, I will go into more detail about optimization dos and don'ts. But right now what is important to know is that no matter the size of the company, the data can still be terrible when it is first exported from a website.

Google Shopping can level the playing field if you put in the effort to optimize your product feed. The data feed, by nature, splits or segments different data points, so you will need to tweak some fields so that they stand on their own.

Many companies do not know how or choose not to put forth the effort to optimize their product feed. When you take the knowledge from this book and apply it to your product feed, you will be able to compete with the big companies.

You do not need a big budget; you just need to be willing to put in the work. With a little time and effort, you can make your product stand out from the rest.

It is no secret that Google loves data. The more data you can provide, the better Google can serve its users. And when it comes to product data, they want it to be fresh and accurate. That is why it is so important to spend time getting your product data feed correct in the beginning. A well-crafted data feed is the foundation of a successful Google Shopping campaign.

If you have a less than optimal "crappy" data feed, you will most likely get less than satisfactory "crappy" results from your ads. I use the word "crappy" because that will be how you will feel about the results. But if you take the time to get it right, you will be rewarded with a better return on your investment from your Google Shopping campaigns. So do not skimp on the data feed setup—it will be worth it in the long run!

Who Needs this Book?

If you are a Shopify store owner or manager, or if you own or manage any other type of eCommerce store, then the information in this book will be invaluable to you. Paid search agencies and online marketers will also benefit. Getting your products live on Google Shopping is one of the best ways to increase your sales and reach a wider audience. This book will show you how to create product listings that are optimized for Google Shopping, how to submit your listings for approval, and how to troubleshoot any problems that you may encounter along the way. In addition, I will provide the best practices for managing your listings on an ongoing basis. Whether you are new to Google Shopping or you have been using it for a while, this book will help you make the most of this powerful platform.

I am here to tell you that creating an amazing product feed does not have to be complicated. In fact, the process can be simple depending on how the feed is created. By following a few simple steps, you can get your products live on Google with minimal effort.

But like anything worth doing in life, there is no substitute for hard work and dedication. It takes a bit of work to get a truly good feed, but the rewards of having your products live on Google are well worth the effort.

Why Optimize?

If you are selling or planning to sell products online, you need to make sure your product feed is optimized for Google Shopping. This is because Google Shopping is one of the most popular ways for people to find and compare products. By optimizing your product feed, you can beat the competitors and ensure that your products are more likely to be seen by potential customers. This, in turn, can lead to more sales and more customers.

There are several things you need to do to optimize your product feed. In this book, I will cover best practices and some not-so-well-known but equally important ways to optimize your products. If you follow my steps, then you will be well on your way to success in Google Shopping.

As an eCommerce business, it is important to always be testing and experimenting to ensure that you are optimizing your product feed for the best possible results. This can seem daunting, but it does not have to be. I will cover a few key things to keep in mind when testing that will help make the process smoother and more effective.

Why does Google Shopping Matter?

With the ever-changing landscape of digital marketing, it can be difficult for small business owners to keep up. Google Shopping is a powerful tool that can help businesses reach new customers, but it can be tricky to master. This book provides a step-by-step guide to getting started with Google Shopping, from setting up your account to optimizing your listings. With clear instructions and practical advice, this book will help you make the most of Google Shopping and take your business to the next level.

Chapter Two

Google Merchant Center

Google Merchant Center (GMC) is a platform for retailers who want to advertise their products on Google Shopping. It can be difficult to use, however, because how it works is not always clear. In this chapter, I will provide a detailed explanation of GMC and show you how to set up your account. By the end of this chapter, you should have a good understanding of what GMC is, and how to start the set-up process.

What is Google Merchant Center?

Google Merchant Center is a platform that allows retailers to upload their product information to Google and make it available for shoppers. It is the first step in setting up a Google Shopping campaign, as it ensures that your products will be eligible to appear in Shopping ads.

It is the central place where retailers manage their:

- store information

- products

- performance

- marketing

- growth

I have chosen to start with Google Merchant Center because Google has pretty much dictated the de facto product feed format for the industry. While there were data feeds being built for other destinations before Google, almost all affiliates, comparison shopping engines, and marketplaces accept the Google product feed format. Therefore, it makes sense to start with a good understanding of GMC and then move on to the setup and actual build of a data feed. Once you have built a feed formatted for Google to accept, it can be sent directly to most platforms, or it will take a small amount of additional effort to create a new feed formatted for the destination of your choice. You will find that most of the product feed formats are similar.

Now that I have covered the basics of Google Merchant Center, I will take a more in-depth look at each of these components. We will start with setting up your account.

How to set up your Google Merchant Center account

If you do not already have a Merchant Center account, setting one up is simple. Just go to merchantcenter.google.com and click "Sign up."

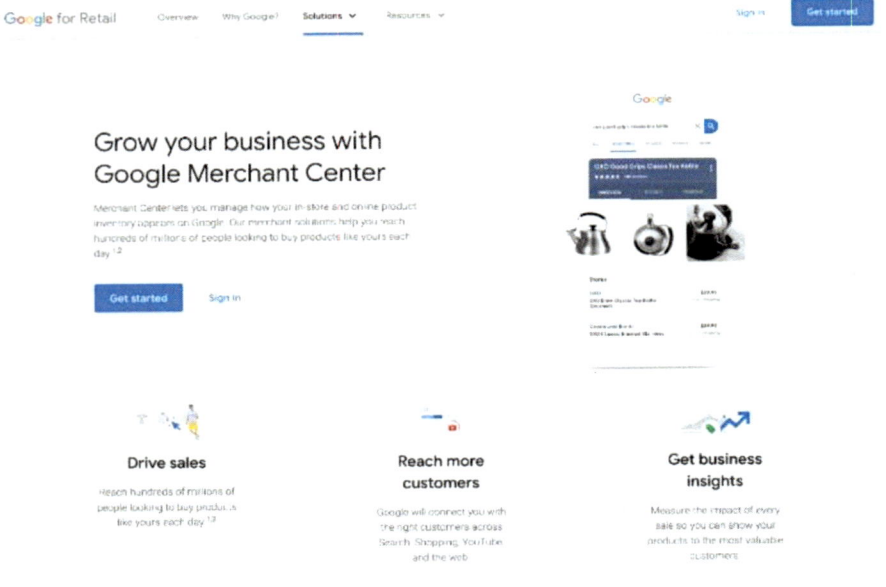

Get your products on Google with Merchant Center

You will be prompted to sign in with your Google account, after which you will be asked to provide basic information about your business. The following chapters will cover in detail each of the different settings and options available in GMC.

Is Google Merchant Center Free?

Yes. There is no charge to set up and use Google Merchant Center. The main reason for having an account is usually to run Google's paid version called Shopping Ads, which was formerly known as Product Listing Ads. If you decide to run Google Shopping Ads, you won't be billed in Google Merchant Center but through your Google Ads account. You can choose to utilize your GMC account exclusively for free product listings on the Google Shopping Tab, but note that running Shopping Ads will likely be more effective in terms of getting your products seen by potential customers.

Pro Tip: You want to make sure that you own your GMC. Do not let an agency set up your GMC account and take ownership. You can let an agency manage your account after you create it, but do not let them set it up with their account email when you first launch. It is very difficult to transfer ownership of GMC.

If you do not feel comfortable setting up Google Merchant Center, that is fine. Invite the agency to help manage the account. They will provide you with an email for the invite, and once they accept they can resume the setup. Again, do this after you have created the account!

Google Merchant Center Help

If you need more help with setting up GMC than what is offered in this book, there are several resources available. Google is not the best at providing direct help, but I would start with the Merchant Center Help Center which offers step-by-step guides for common tasks, as well as the FAQs and contact information for support. You can also find helpful tips and tricks on the Merchant Center blog. In addition, there are several online forums where you can ask questions and get advice from other merchants. With a little effort, you should be able to get your Merchant Center account up and running in no time.

Google Merchant Center is a powerful tool that can help you manage your online store and product listings. In the following chapters, I will cover the basics of Google Merchant Center and some of the key features that you should be aware of. I will also discuss some of the lesser-known features that you may not need to use on a day-to-day basis. By the end of this guide, you will have a firm understanding of how to use Google Merchant Center to its full potential.

Chapter Three

GMC Account Setting

The Google Merchant Center is a powerful tool for online retailers, as it provides access to a variety of features that can help to streamline operations and boost sales. One of the most important areas of the Merchant Center is the account settings area. This is where you will find the content Application Programming Interface (API), general account settings, linked accounts, and more. Except for the content API, each of these settings should be filled in or activated prior to launching your first product. By taking the time to set up your account properly, you can ensure that your store runs smoothly and avoid any potential problems down the road.

To access the account settings, click the tools icon at the top of the page

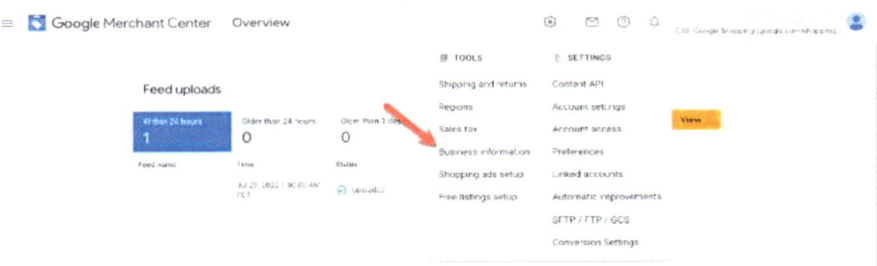

I will review each of the settings below, explaining what they are, and let you know which information is important to fill out.

Account Settings

Time Zone and Language

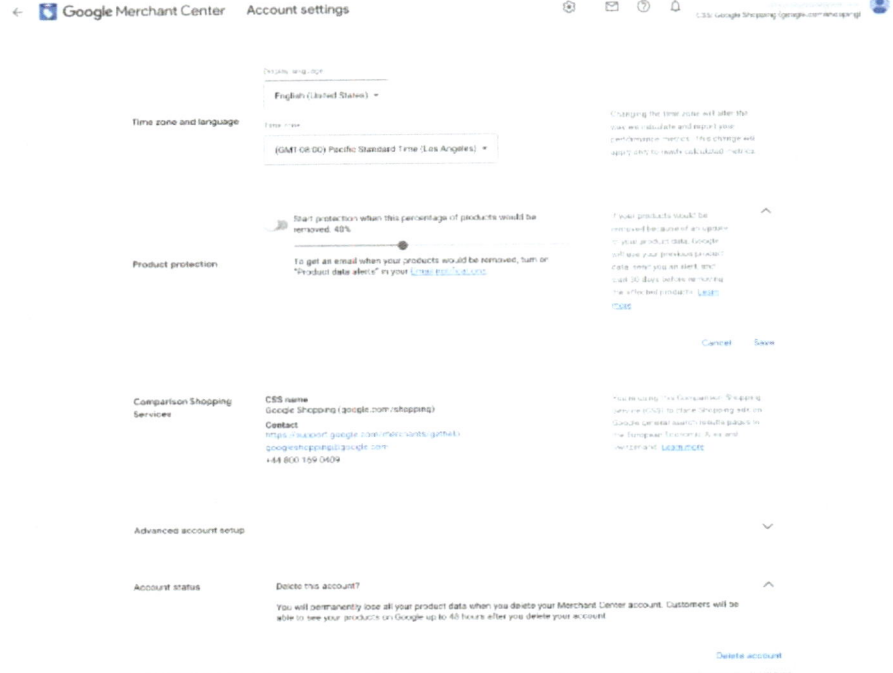

You will find the settings for language and time zone in the account settings. I recommend setting both to your local time zone and language so that you can easily understand the interface and be sure that all dates are accurate.

The most common reason I look at the time stamp within GMC is when I am checking the most recent feed update. If the time zone is different than the one you are in, you must convert or change the hours to your time zone while checking. If you can remove the potential for error by setting the correct time zone, then you should. It may save you some headache later if you or someone else misinterprets the time!

Product Protection

The next section is product protection, which monitors the percentage of products coming into Merchant Center. I would enable this and set it for 10%. The default is 40% which I feel is too high. This setting will send you an alert if the threshold is exceeded. For example, if we have 200 products in our daily product feed and 25 products were removed in the next delivered feed, we will receive an alert if we have set the threshold for 10% or 20 products. Wouldn't you want to know if 10% or more of your business is suddenly not available to purchase by the public?

Comparison Shopping Services

For users in the European Union, there is an additional service that can be used for comparison shopping. This service is a result of a lawsuit against Google to make the Google Shopping channel more competitive. This allows comparison shopping services to bid on shopping ads on behalf of a merchant they represent. There is more to it than this, but it is not relevant for those living outside of the European Union. However, for users in the EU, this service can be used to find the best deals on products and retailers have gotten used to working with it.

Advance Account Setup

This section can be ignored by 99% of users. This is used by agencies or by a company with millions of products that require more than one Merchant Center. The advanced account allows you to see multiple GMC accounts within one login.

Account Status

Would you like to delete your Merchant Center account? This is where you would do it. Be careful, as you will permanently lose all your product data within 48 hours if you delete your account.

Account Access

The account access settings in Google Merchant Center allow you to give or revoke access to your Merchant Center account. This is helpful if you need to share your GMC account with another person, such as an agency or a colleague. You can also revoke access if you no longer need it.

There are two ways to access Google Merchant Center: Users and Email contacts. The difference between a user and an email contact is that a user has a login and password to access your Merchant Center account, while an email contact does not. Email contacts can only receive emails about your Merchant Center account.

If you decide to give someone access to your Merchant Center account, you can choose what level of access they have: Owner, Full Access, and Read Only. The owner gives the person full control of the account and all its settings. Full Access allows the person to make changes to the account, but they cannot change the account settings. Read Only gives the person view-only access to the account and they cannot make any changes.

To give someone account access, go to the Account Access tab in Google Merchant Center and click Add User or Add Email Contact. Enter the person's email address and select the level of access you want them to have. Then click Add. The person will then receive an email with instructions on how to log in or confirm their email address (for email contacts).

Preferences

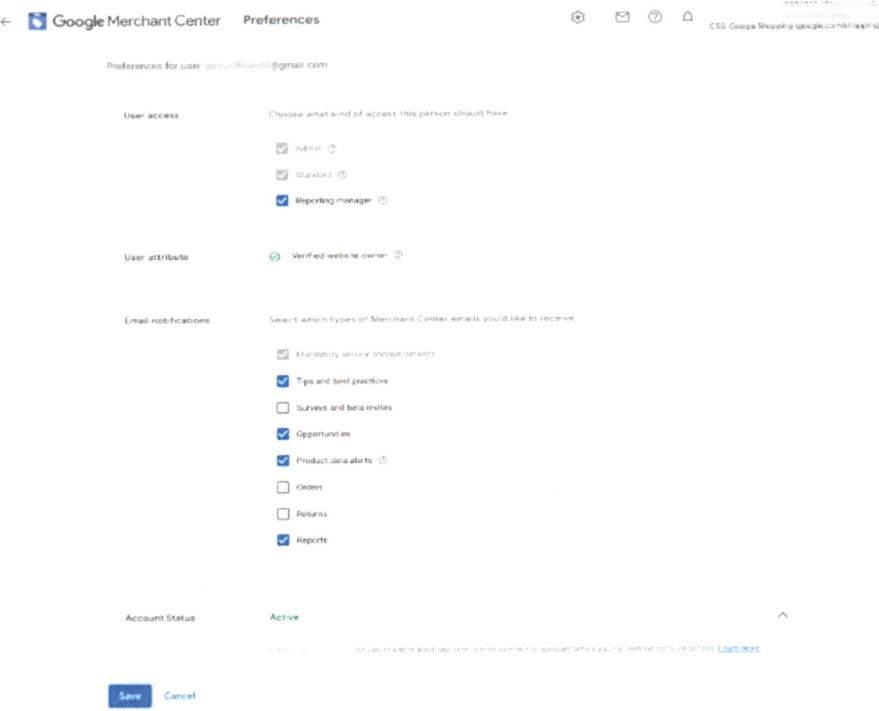

The preferences settings in Google Merchant Center allow you to customize your experience with the tool. There are a few options that are worth mentioning. This is where you can choose to receive email notifications for various things happening in your Merchant Center account. For example, you can choose to receive email notifications when you have orders and returns or when a product is removed from your feed.

More importantly, you can also check to see if you are the verified website owner.

This is particularly helpful when there is a question about which email owns or has previously verified the website. If you were to log in with the email in question and check the preferences, you will immediately know if it is associated with the verified website owner.

I recommend turning on all the notifications, as you will want to know if there are any issues with your product data or if your account is suspended.

Linked Accounts

Google Ads

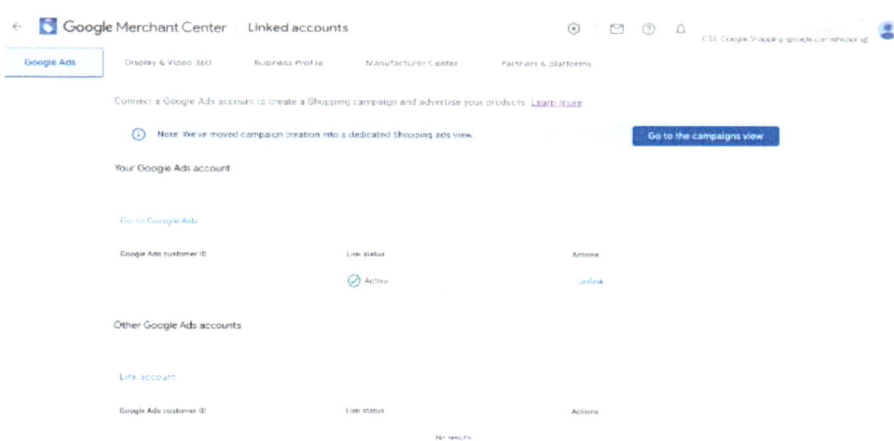

When you set up your product data feed, you may be eligible for Google's free listings. There are a number of requirements that need to be met to make sure your products are on free listings, but we will discuss that in another section.

If you wish to advertise with Google ads, you will need to link a Google Ads account with GMC. When you approve a link between your Google Ads and Merchant Center accounts, the data from one will flow into another so that it can be used in advertising campaigns.

Depending on which type of product information is submitted to them (e.g. Shopping), different types of advertisement may become available for sale or display via dynamic remarketing techniques (such as retargeting users after they have visited your website).

Display & Video 360

Google Display & Video 360 is a tool that helps you with programmatic advertising on a demand-side platform (DSP). With this tool, you can create campaigns to show your products to people, and you can also use dynamic remarketing to show people ads for your products on websites they visit.

While Google Display Video is a powerful tool, it can be complex, so I recommend avoiding this type of advertising until you have outgrown Google ads. You will know when you have reached that stage when your product line has expanded, and you need to reach a wider audience than what Google ads can provide. Until then, stick to simpler advertising methods.

Business Profile

This information should have been filled in earlier in the business profile section in Google Merchant Center where you put information about your company. If the business profile owner is the administrator of the GMC account, most likely this will automatically be filled in. You may need to click on the "link account" button to activate this.

Manufacturer Center

Google Manufacturer Center is for brands that manufacture their own products. This platform can provide customers with up-to-date and authoritative product info that will help them find their next purchase. Like a retailer selling their product from Google Merchant Center, it can help expand brand awareness whenever shoppers are searching for items on google.

This is not a platform for most retailers even if you are creating your own products. Stick with Google Merchant Center. You will thank me!

Partners & Platforms

This section of Google Merchant Center is used to link eCommerce store builders, payment and shipping providers, data feed apps, and more. Usually, you do not need to do anything here unless a linking partner provides instructions.

It is good to occasionally review this section to make sure linked partners are still active. If they are no longer active, I would recommend removing them. You do not want someone to have continued access to your account after you have terminated the business relationship.

Automatic Improvements

Auto-improvements are settings that can be turned on for your Google Merchant Center account. With this setting enabled, Google will automatically make changes to your product listings to help you sell more products and improve customer experience. I recommend keeping this setting enabled so that you can benefit from these ongoing improvements. If at any time you would like to disable auto-improvements, you can do so by editing your account settings.

Automatic Updates

Automatic item updates can help keep your product data accurate. Sometimes, product data on your website can become outdated—product information, such as price and availability, changes frequently. If you have the "Automatic item updates" setting turned on in your Merchant Center account, Google will automatically update this information in your Google Shopping ads, so you do not have to. This way, customers will always see the most accurate information about your products.

Some of the changes that may be made include:

- Price

- Availability

- Condition

With automatic improvements enabled, you can:

- Save time by not having to manually update your product data.

- Ensure that customers always see the most accurate info about your products.

- Improve customer experience.

- Emotional benefits:

    a. Having an automatically updated account gives you peace of mind.

    b. Knowing that your account is being constantly improved makes you feel confident in using GMC.

A word of warning: do not use automatic item updates as a replacement for regular feed updates. Think of this as a temporary fix for when there is a problem with the price or availability.

Pro Tip: if you notice frequent automatic updates being made to your products, look for an opportunity to change your feed schedule to more closely align with when website changes are made. Many times, I have seen where website updates are being made after the feed is being sent out. I recommend sending your feed to google at least 30 minutes after your scheduled website changes. Sometimes schedules can vary a little and you want some room for error.

Automatic Image Improvements

This is one of the more exciting features. Often there are images with promotional overlays on them. For example, retailers like to put a sale sticker on a product image to draw attention to a sale. It can be difficult to remove the sale sticker between the website and GMC for it is often forgotten. Google will disallow the product if it has this type of overlay on the image. Automatic image improvements will remove the offending overlay and leave the product image intact. Pretty cool, huh?

Google does warn that the improvement may not always work. They mentioned that sometimes the promotional overlay cannot be removed, or part of the product image could be altered. If you see that Google has applied an image improvement to your account, I would do a quick check to make sure it looks okay.

SFTP/FTP/GCS

SFTP/FTP

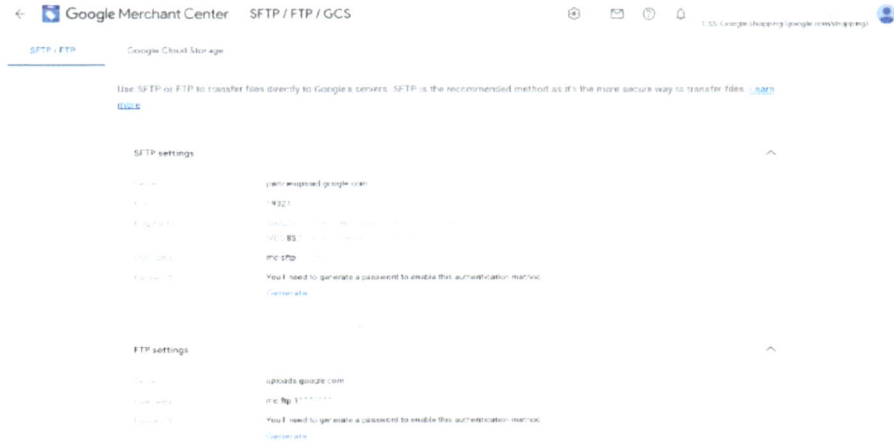

If you need to set up a file transfer protocol (FTP) to transfer your files to GMC, this is where you input the credentials to accomplish this. You will need the URL, username, and password. It's a good idea to save these credentials somewhere for future access. While it is not difficult to create a new password, each time the password is changed you need to make changes to the platform sending the file via SFTP or FTP. As mentioned elsewhere, make sure that the schedule for the file upload is after your daily website updates. You want to capture these changes as soon as you can. Otherwise, you may get flagged for incorrect data.

Google Cloud Storage

It's worth noting that files can be stored in Google Cloud Storage and Google can retrieve the data for Google Merchant Center. This is a more advanced process, and I would not recommend this for the average retailer.

Conversion Settings

When you sell products through GMC there are basically two channels within Google that are used: paid or free.

When you use the paid channel, Google Ads, you set up tracking within Google Ads and can track sales quite easily.

Up until recently, when products were sold through the free channel you had no easy way to track the sales. Wouldn't you want to know if products were selling on the free channel? Obviously, the answer is yes. There was a workaround where you could add tracking to the link (product page URL) in the feed and that would be changed by Google AdWords if the product was going through the paid channel. This was not easy to apply for most retailers.

Well, Google has finally given us a more direct way to track sales on the free channel. This can be done by enabling auto-tagging within the Merchant Center. You need to link your account to Google Analytics and/or Shopify to have this feature work.

Inside the Conversions settings tab, toggler the Auto-tagging button to "ON".

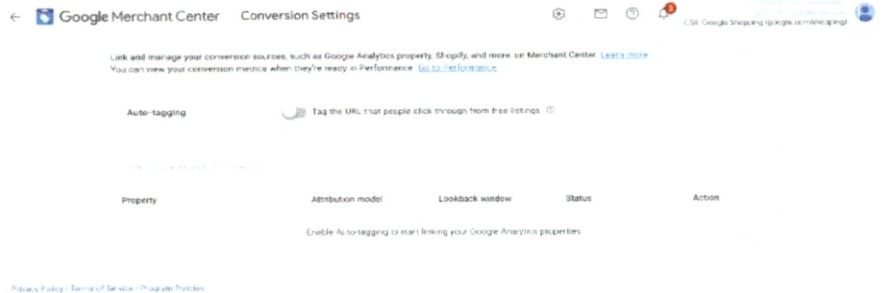

Pro Tip: This setting should absolutely be turned on. The outcome will be better tracking and attribution of your sales through Google Shopping.

Content API

The content API in Google Merchant Center is another way for you to submit product data to Google. Google recommends this method if you have a lot of products, or if your product offerings change frequently. You can think of this as a direct connection between Google Merchant Center and your store's website. Each time a product is changed on the website, the product will be updated almost instantly in GMC with the most recent change. As you can see, the Google Shopping API is automated and quick. It is technically complex for the average store owner, but third-party vendors/applications often take advantage of this feature which lessens the burden and makes it accessible for most who want it.

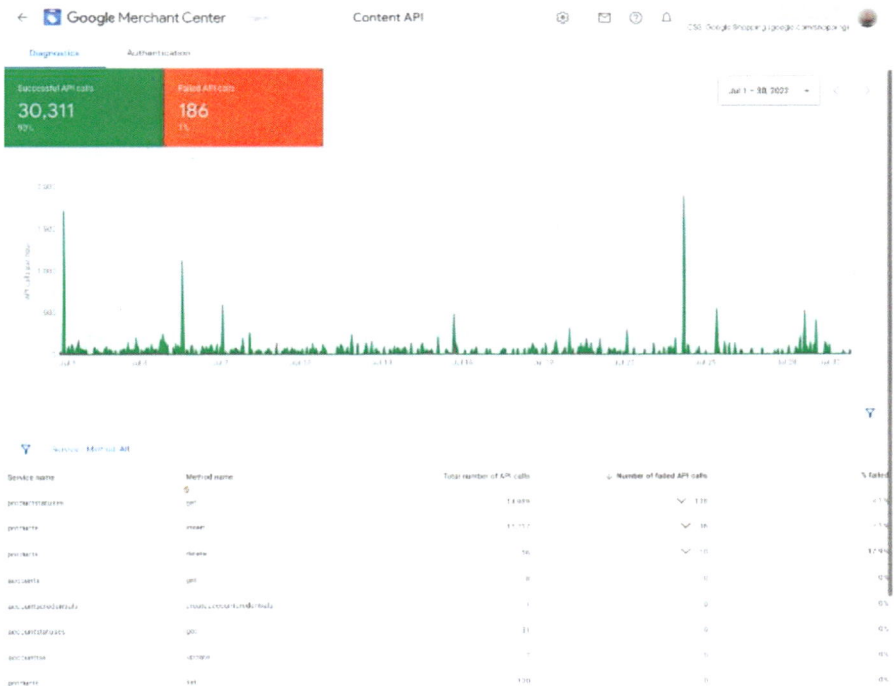

If you are taking advantage of the Content API, generally there is not much for a retailer to do in this part of GMC. Think of this area as a reporting interface where you can periodically check on the status of the API to make sure that updates are flowing through correctly.

Usually, an easy way to determine if the API is working correctly is that if you know that new products are being added to the store, you should check the products area of Merchant Center and look for the increased product count there. If you see that it has been updated correctly, you do not have to worry too much about checking the Content API.

Chapter Four

GMC Account Tools

In the tools tab, you can specify your business information, such as your website URL, country, and currency. You'll also need to set up your tax and shipping settings here. This is very important information, and I will go over each of these in detail.

To access the account tools, click the tools icon at the top of the page.

Business Information

The business information tab is where you enter your company's contact information, such as your website URL, address, and phone number. You'll also need to enter your company's country and currency. This information is used by Google to verify your company and determine which taxes and shipping settings to use.

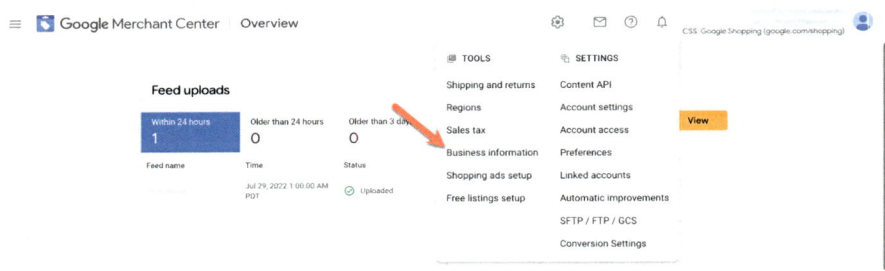

Once you have clicked on the business information link you should see the following screen:

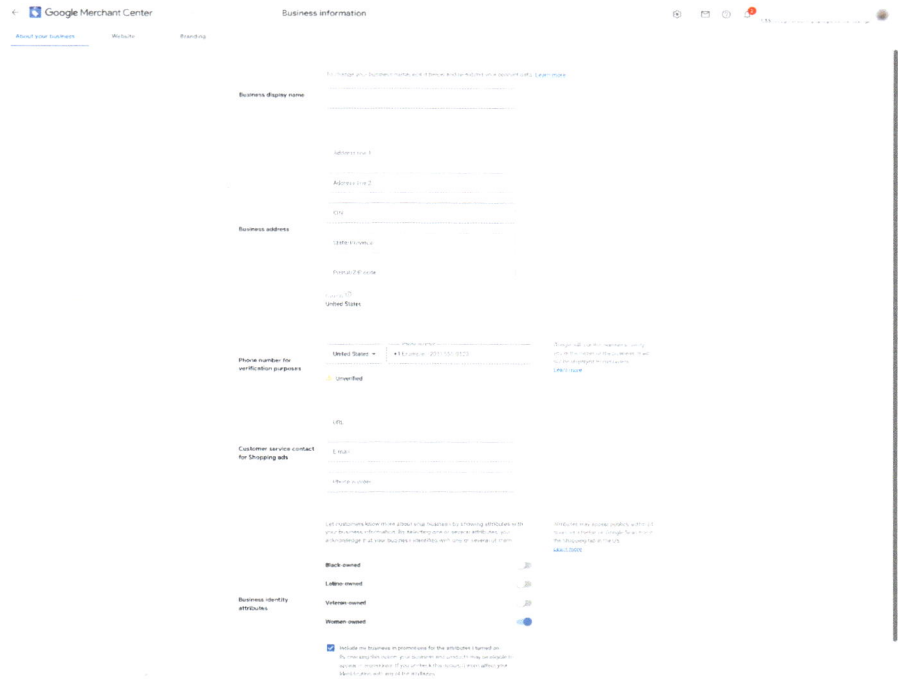

In the about your business tab fill out the following:

Business display name

This is the name of your store or shop. This displays to the customer so most likely you will want it to match your website store name.

Business address

Fill out this entire section.

Phone number for verification purposes

Google will use this number to verify business ownership. It is not displayed to the customer.

Customer Service Contact for Shopping ads

At the very least fill out the email in this section. If you have a contact page on your website, you can add this. If you also have a phone number for support, you may add this as well.

Business identity attributes

For businesses that qualify as Black-owned, Latino-owned, or veteran-owned, adding the appropriate attributes can be beneficial. Google displays badges in the search and shopping tabs reflecting the business' identity attributes. There is a growing population that cares about this and will patronize businesses because of this. Adding these badges can help businesses tap into this market and attract new customers. Furthermore, these badges can also help build trust with potential customers and create a sense of loyalty. In today's competitive marketplace, any advantage that a business can have is worth exploring. Consequently, businesses that qualify for any of these identity attributes should consider adding them to their Google listings.

Website

Under the website tab, is where you will need to verify and claim your store's website URL.

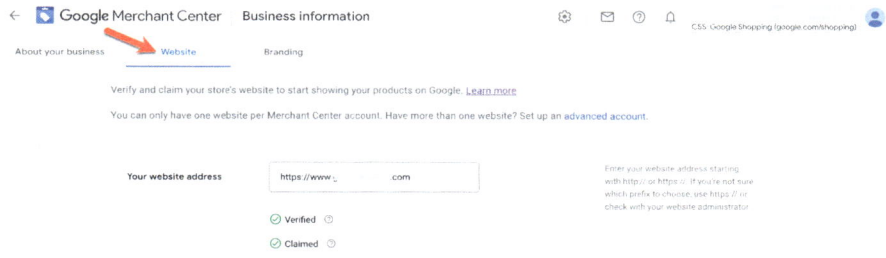

The reason Google does this is for security purposes. You don't want someone else to claim that they are your store or brand and try to sell products online by misrepresenting themselves as you. There are two steps to this process.

1. Add your website address. You need to put in the URL that matches your store. For example, if you are a secure website and use SSL (secure sockets layer), you would start with HTTPS and then your URL - https:/widgetstore.com.

> *Pro Tip:* If you are a Shopify store, you may need to add the prefix "shop" to the URL, e.g., https://shop.widgetstore.com. Check the URL that is exported from Shopify to determine the correct structure. You will need to match whatever the URL is in the feed.

2. Verify your website by one of the following four methods.

a. Upload an HTML file—if you choose this method, Google will create an HTML file for you to upload to your website. This is not visible to customers and only used for Google verification.

b. Add an HTML tag—if this method is chosen, google will provide you with an HTML tag to add to the header of your website. This is also not visible to the customer and Google will use this for verification.

c. Google tag manager—if you are using Google tag manager then you can install a code snippet onto your website. See Google for more information on this process. You should be familiar with Google tag manager before trying this.

d. Google Analytics—if you are using Google Analytics and you have edit permissions in the account then you can implement the verification this way. All that needs to be done is the make sure that the Google Analytics global site tag* is implemented. *As of this writing, Google Analytics will be shut down in July 2023 and there is no update if GA4 (the new version of Google Analytics) will be used.

Once you've chosen one of the above four methods, you'll click the "claim website" button at the bottom right. Only the user who has started the set-up can verify the website.

Sometimes Google will have enough information to verify your website and the URL will be automatically verified. This will occur once you add the website address in the business information section and you click continue.

Branding

Branding is one of the most important aspects of any business. It's what customers remember you by, and it can make or break a company. That's why it's so important to get branding right from the start.

The branding tab in the Google Merchant Center is a great way to make sure your company's branding is front and center.

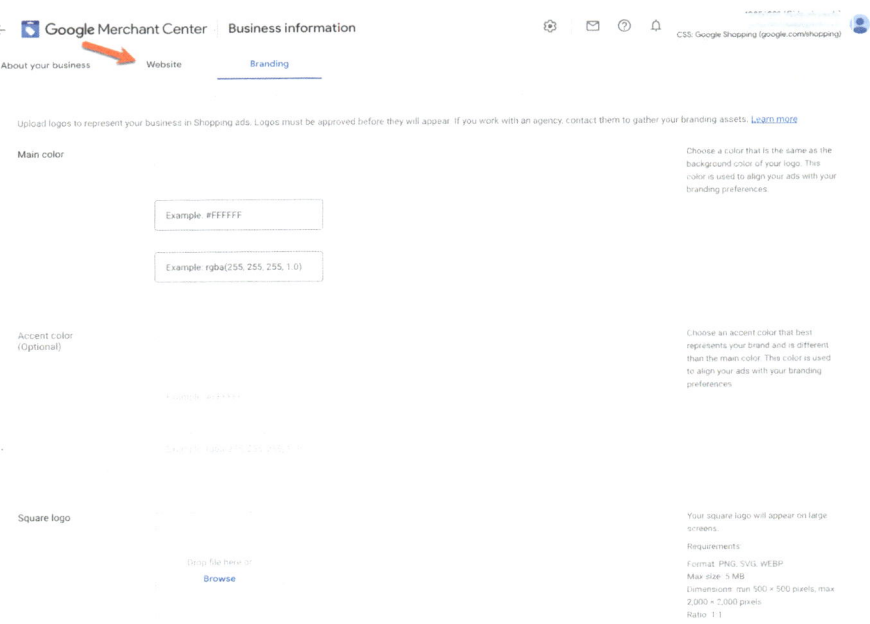

You can upload your logo and add a main color and accent color which can show on ads.

All of this helps to create a consistent brand experience for your customers, no matter where they see your products. So, if you're looking to boost your brand, start with the branding tab in the Google Merchant Center.

Shipping and returns

Who gives a ship? Your customer! But what good is all the work you have done to get your product listed if you don't get your product to your customer efficiently? Shipping is also one of the factors that people consider when they are deciding whether to buy. So, let's get your ship together and get it set up right!

The shipping and returns section of Google Merchant Center is where you specify your shipping and return policies. You'll need to set up your shipping rates and methods here, as well as specify any restrictions on returns. Make sure to be clear and concise in your policies, so that your customers know what to expect.

You can choose from a variety of shipping services, including:

- Standard shipping

- Expedited shipping

- Express shipping

- Overnight shipping

- Worldwide shipping

Add a shipping service

1. Click on the "+Add shipping service" link

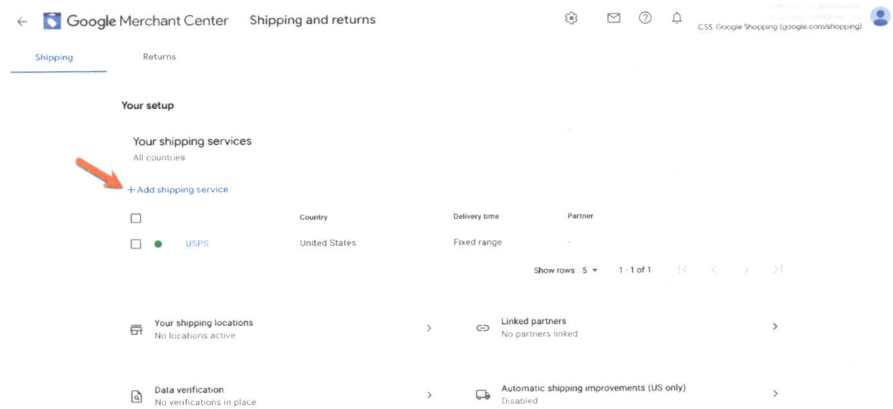

2. Fill in the shipping service name, choose the country and the currency, and leave the delivery location "at the customer's address."

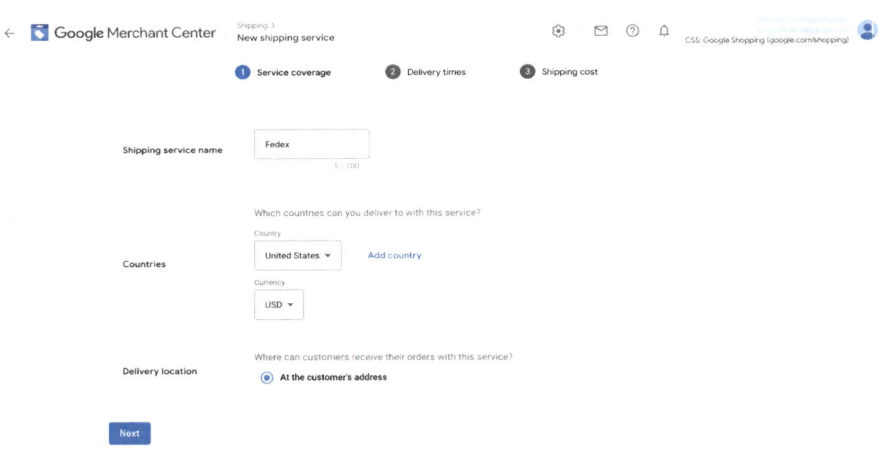

3. You choose the delivery time based on a shipping partner or you can set a range of delivery times. You will need to have a "ship from location," which is usually your store, warehouse location, or wherever you are shipping from.

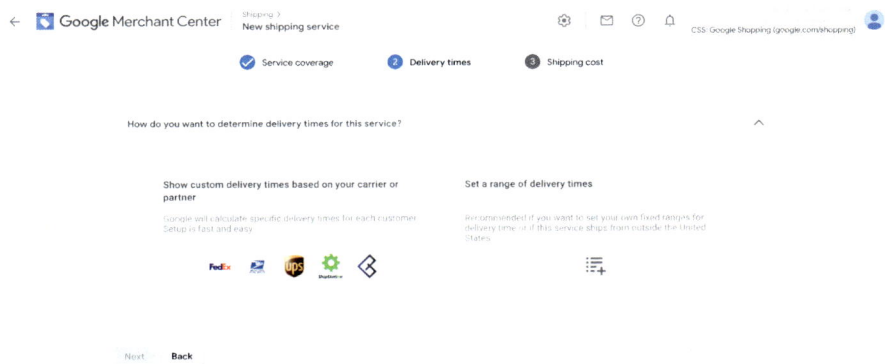

4. In this example, I have chosen FedEx 2 day shipping

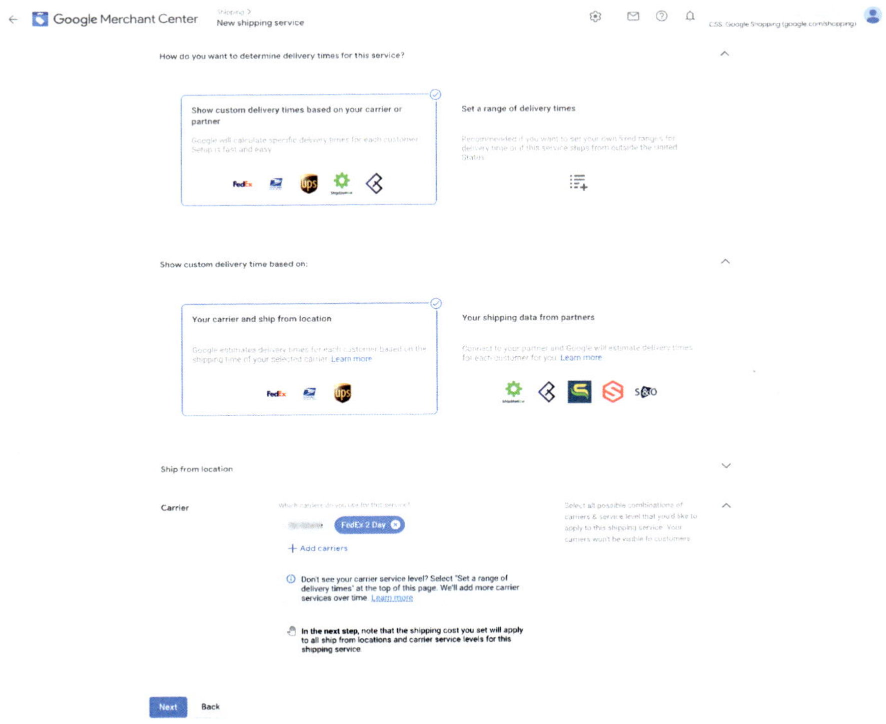

If you decide to choose "set a range of delivery times" in step 3 above you would do the following:

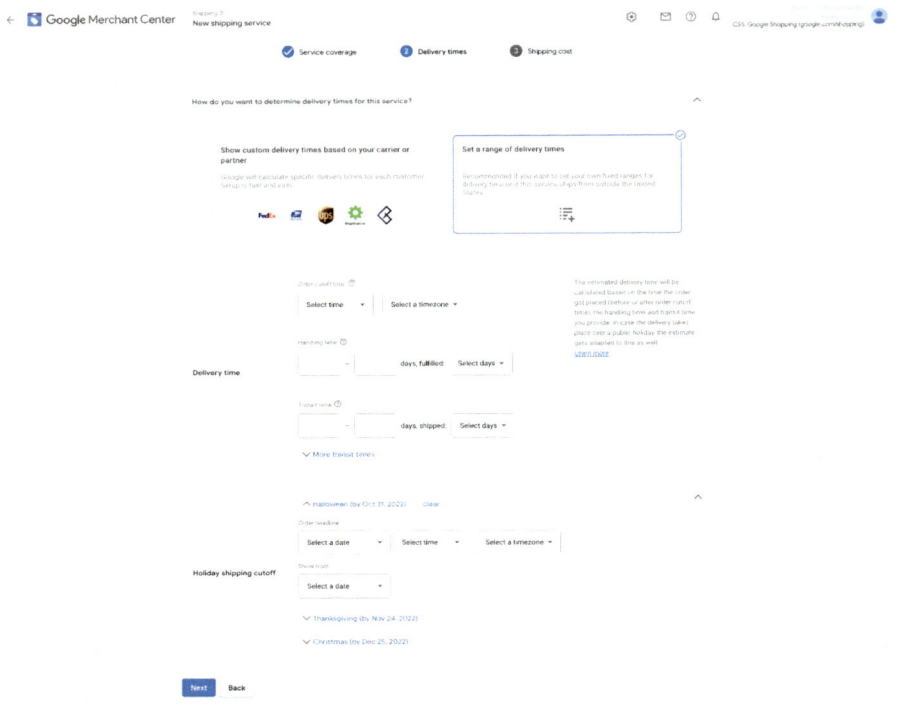

Choose the time of day by which an order must be placed to start being processed the same day (cutoff time).

Enter the minimum and the maximum number of business days required for processing an order (handling time).

Add the number of business days the entire service can possibly take (transit time).

In the US, Australia, and France you can set the transit time based on regions. Click on "More transit times" to use regions.

Optional Advanced Settings

You can add a minimum order value for a shipping service if you have a minimum order threshold on your store website.

You can set holiday shipping cutoffs for orders. This is a great way to set expectations upfront and reduce customer service issues due to missed shipping deadlines.

5. Lastly, set the shipping cost.

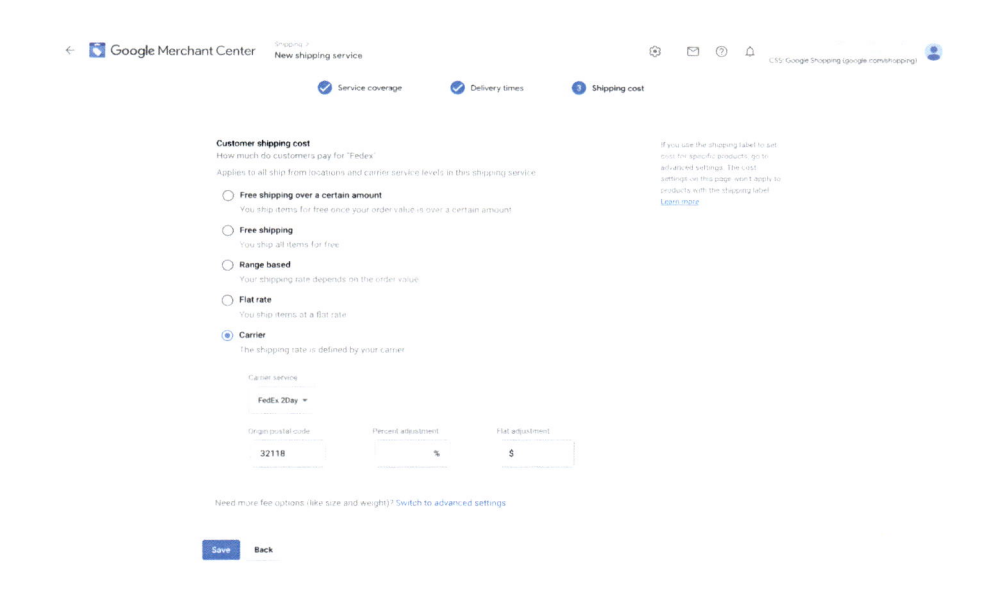

Pro Optimization Tip: it is ideal if you can offer free shipping for your product. This will keep you the most competitive and consumer friendly. Most retailers adjust the price to help make up for the free shipping offer. I've also found that a very low flat rate also works well. A $1—$3 shipping rate usually is successful. This allows you to offer free shipping as an incentive during the holidays or a sale.

Your Shipping Locations

Your shipping locations are where you ship your products from. This is usually your store or warehouse location, but it can be anywhere that ships your products to customers. You'll need to specify the shipping addresses for each location.

    To add a ship from location:

    Click on the "+new location" link

    Enter the name of the location, street address, city, state/province, and country.

Enter the handling time and order cutoff time.
Click on "save."

Linked Partners

Linked partners are companies that you have partnered with to provide shipping services.

Data Verification

Data verification is a process that Google uses to ensure the accuracy of the shipping information that you provide. By linking one of the shipping partners to your merchant center account, Google will compare the data that you submit with the data from a shipping partner, therefore improving the accuracy of the delivery times shown to your customers.

ShipStation, CedCommerce, Simprosys, ShipHero, and Sales & Orders are some of the shipping software providers that integrate with Google Merchant Center. They help to automate the shipping process, make it easier for you to manage your orders and close the loop for shipping data verification.

Automatic Shipping Improvements

Google Merchant Center offers several features to help streamline the shipping process for online sellers. One such feature is automatic shipping improvements. This allows Google to compare the data that you submit with the data from a shipping partner, thereby improving the accuracy of the delivery times shown to your customers.

You may be asking yourself why would I want to enable this feature? By showing more accurate delivery times, especially if they are faster, you will typically see better conversion rates. Remember, you are constantly battling Amazon Prime's two-day shipping and many customers use this as the benchmark for delivery!

Google uses several factors when considering an estimated delivery time. These may include:

- current handling time and shipping time settings.

- the delivery postal code of an order.

- whether it's a weekday or a weekend when the order was placed.

- and parcel tracking data.

At the time of this writing, Automatic Shipping Improvements are only available in the US.

Your Metrics

The Metrics section of Google Merchant Center is where you can track your shipping performance. You can see how many orders were shipped on time, late, or canceled. You can also see:

- the average shipping time for all your orders.

- the percentage of products with shipping costs.

- the percentage of products with delivery times.

Recommendations

The Recommendations section of Google Merchant Center is where you can find suggestions on how to improve your shipping performance. These recommendations are based on your shipping metrics and are designed to help you improve your shipping times and lower your shipping costs.

Feed Level Shipping

It's possible to configure shipping at the product level within the feed. You would need to include several additional attributes in the feed to accomplish this, such as shipping label, shipping weight, the dimensions such as shipping length, width, height, and transit time label. I'm not suggesting that you use this method, but it is nice to know you have other options.

Sometimes you may have a few products that are unusually large or heavy and they are not able to be shipped via standard shipping methods. Setting shipping parameters inside of the feed can be the simplest method.

Final Thoughts on Shipping

If you have set up shipping in GMC and decide to add shipping attributes in the data feed, the data feed will override the Merchant Center settings. This is good to be aware of when troubleshooting shipping issues.

> *Pro Tip:* The shipping costs you create in GMC must match the shipping costs on your website, otherwise you risk account suspension for incorrect shipping costs. Google will allow you to over-estimate the costs but never underestimate!

If you provide several shipping services for one product, Google will pick the lowest shipping rate for the product and this rate will be shown to customers.

Returns Policy

Your returns policy is where you specify the conditions under which a customer can return an item. You'll need to specify the time limit for returns, as well as any restocking fees that may apply. Make sure to be clear and concise in your policy, so that your customers know what to expect.

How to create a Return Policy

1. Log in to your Google Merchant Center account.
2. Click the Tool icon and then select Shipping and returns.
3. Click on the "Returns" tab at the top.

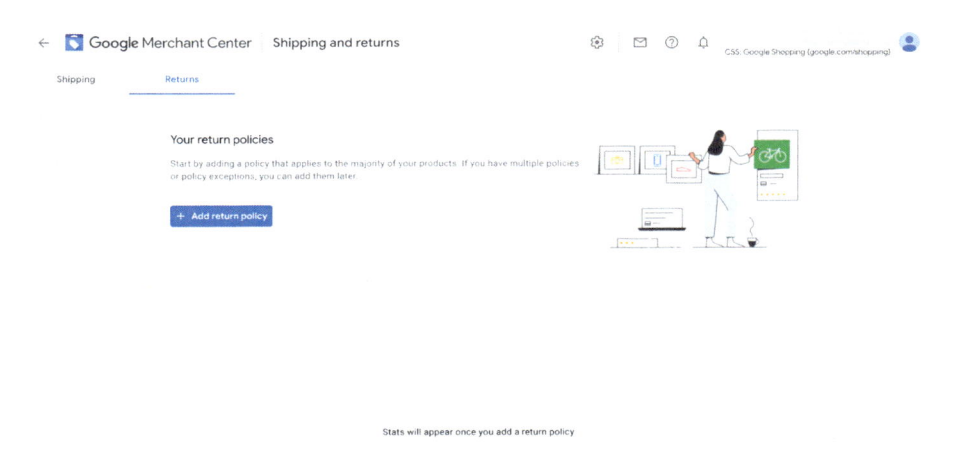

4. Click the Add a new return policy button.
5. Select the country.

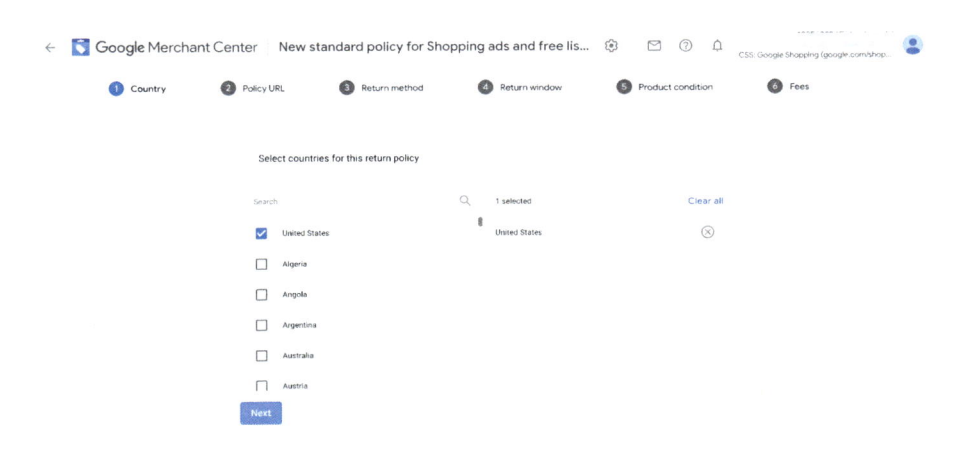

6. Provide the URL of the return policy on your website and select the appropriate option for accepting returns.

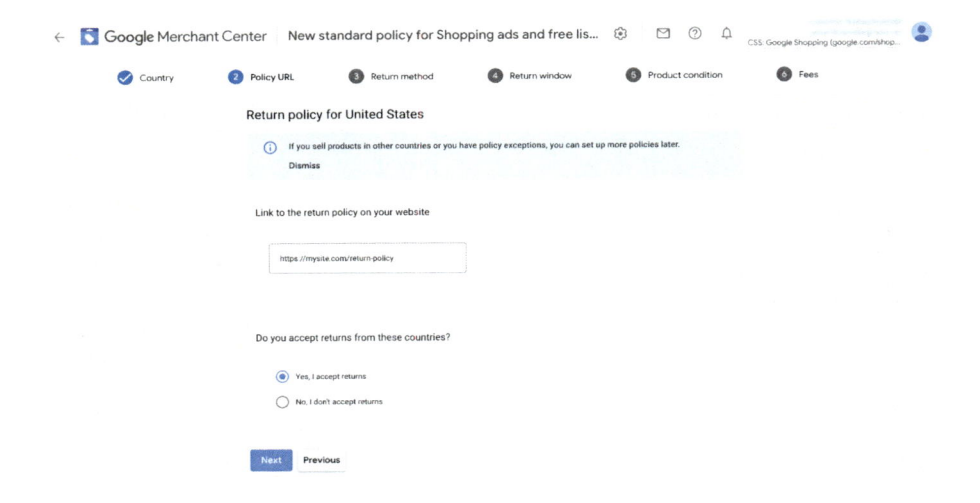

7. Fill in the return method.

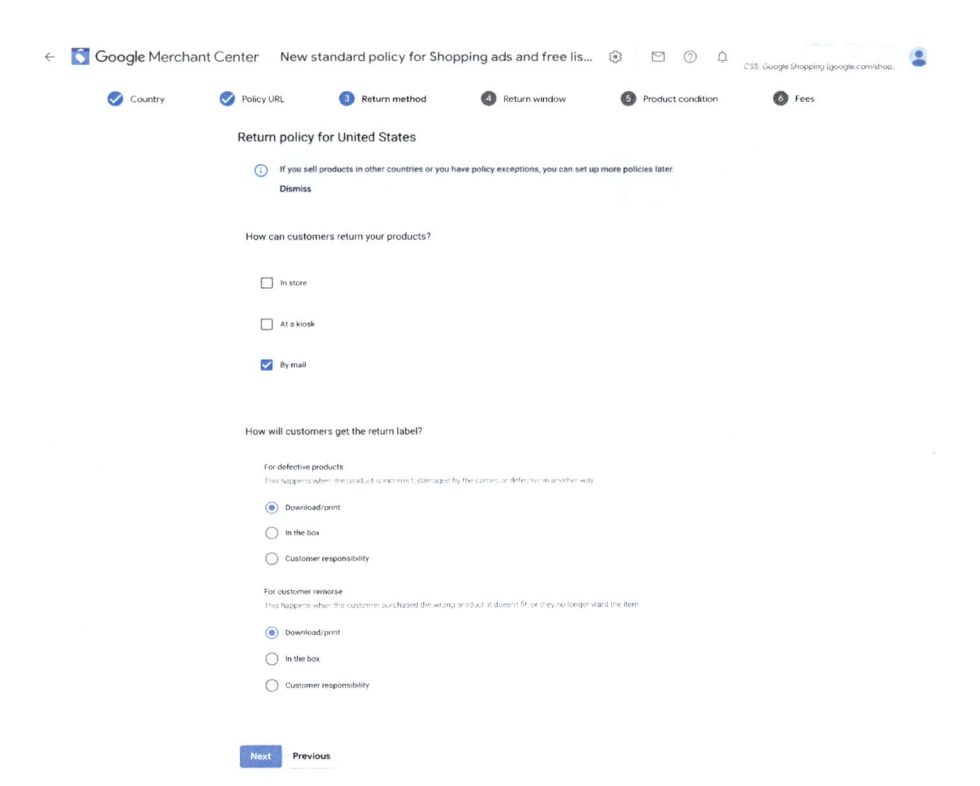

8. Fill in the return window information.

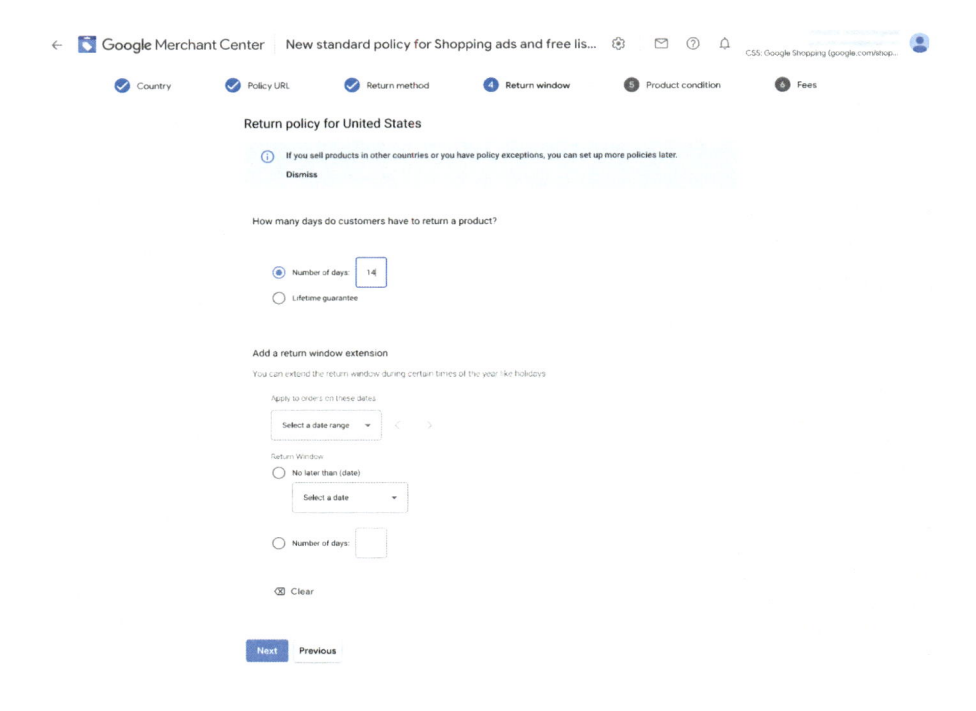

9. Indicate the criteria for the condition of returned products.

10. Lastly, decide if you will charge a restocking fee and charge for return shipping. Review the information and click "Done."

Regions

The regions section found in Google Merchant Center lets you choose where your products will be available to customers in. You can also adjust the price by location. While this feature may be ideal for local inventory ads, it is also available for standard and smart shopping ads.

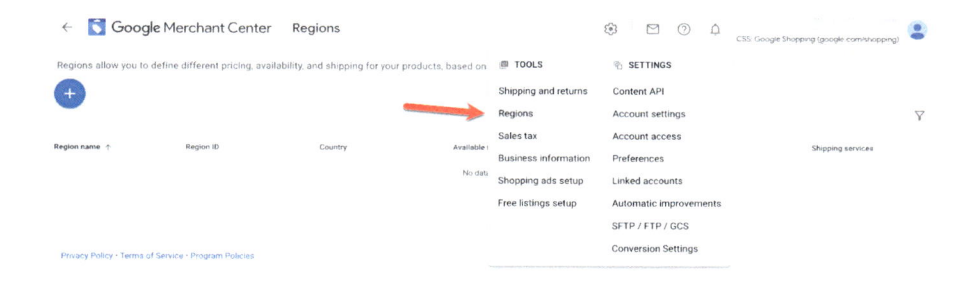

There are a few requirements that must be met to take advantage of regions. They are as follows:

- You must be able to accommodate the region ID parameter passed by Google onto your product landing pages and in turn dynamically show the correct price and availability for that region. This is a sophisticated technique that will likely require a developer. Most out-of-the-box website solutions will not support this feature. This will most likely be the hardest requirement to meet.

- Regions are only supported in the United States, France, Australia, Brazil, and Russia. There may be a few eligible beta countries as well. You would need to check with a Google representative to find out if there are other supported countries.

- The currency used for your region must be the same as the currency used for the initial product listing.

- There is a requirement for regions where the geographic size and population must exceed a certain threshold. You will see an error message shown in the issue column on the regions page if this threshold is not met.

Sales Tax

Tax Settings

Before you can list your products on Google, you need to set up your sales tax information. This is important because shoppers need to know how much they'll be charged in taxes. This section will walk you through the process of setting up sales tax in the Google Merchant Center. Google recommends checking with your tax advisor before setting your tax. This is probably not a bad idea!

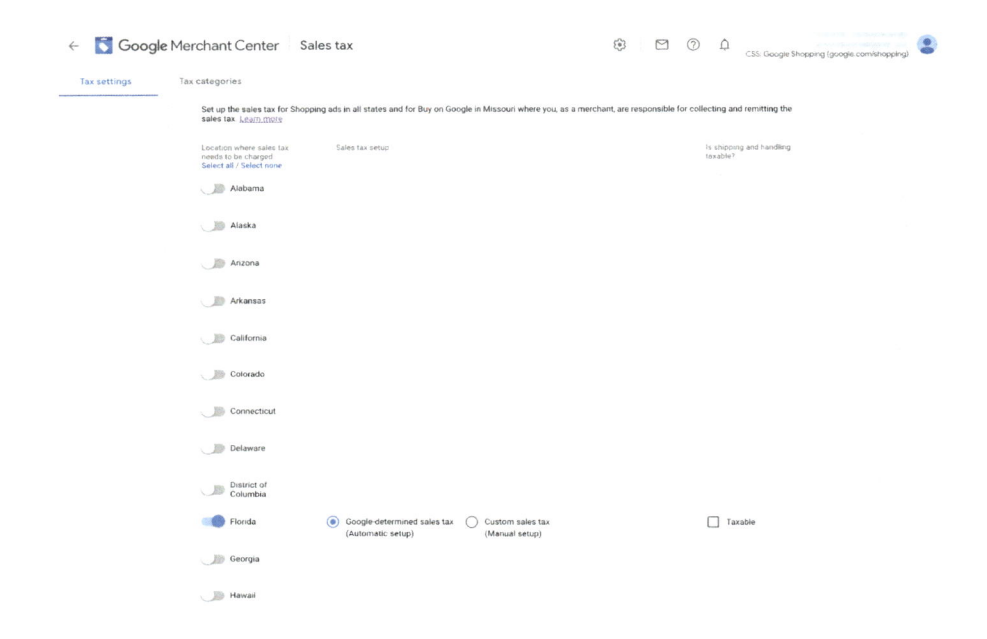

1. Log in to Google Merchant Center.
2. Click on the gear icon in the top right corner and select Settings.
3. Toggle the states where you are required to collect tax. At the very least, you usually need to collect tax in the state your business is located in.

> *Pro Tip:* Make sure to review your website's tax settings to determine if you collect tax on shipping and handling in addition to the price of the item.

> *Pro Tip:* Opt-in to use Google's determined sales tax which is an automatic setup on Google's part. This is a no-brainer! You do not want to

keep up with all the tax requirements throughout the country. Incorrect tax settings are high on the list for account suspensions so you want to get this right.

4. Review your tax information and click "Save."

Tax Categories

The tax category attribute allows you to assign a custom tax rule to a product. This is useful for products that are subject to different tax rates in different jurisdictions.

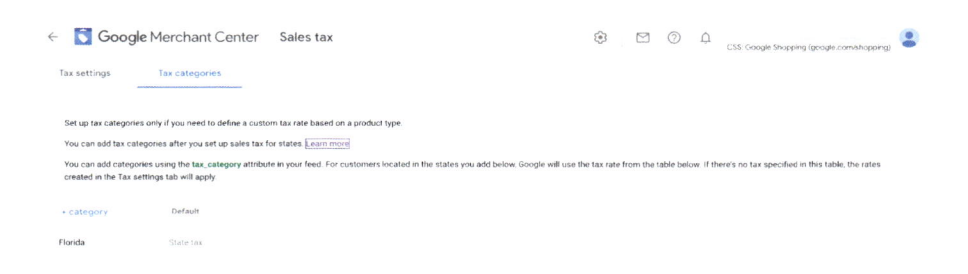

For example, you can use the tax category attribute to exempt certain apparel from tax in some US states and assign a lower tax rate to other products. To do this, simply create a new tax category and then assign it to the appropriate products.

Free Listings Setup

Google offers free product listings for retailers to help customers find the products they're looking for. By taking advantage of this program, retailers can reach potential customers on a variety of platforms, including the Shopping tab, YouTube, Google Search (.com), Google Images, and Google Lens.

Free listings also allow retailers to take advantage of features like product-rich results, which can help their products stand out and drive traffic to their stores.

While there is no charge to list products on Google, retailers are responsible for ensuring that their listings are accurate and up to date. Ultimately, free product listings on Google provide a valuable opportunity for retailers to connect with customers and grow their business.

So how can you tell if a product listing is free or not?

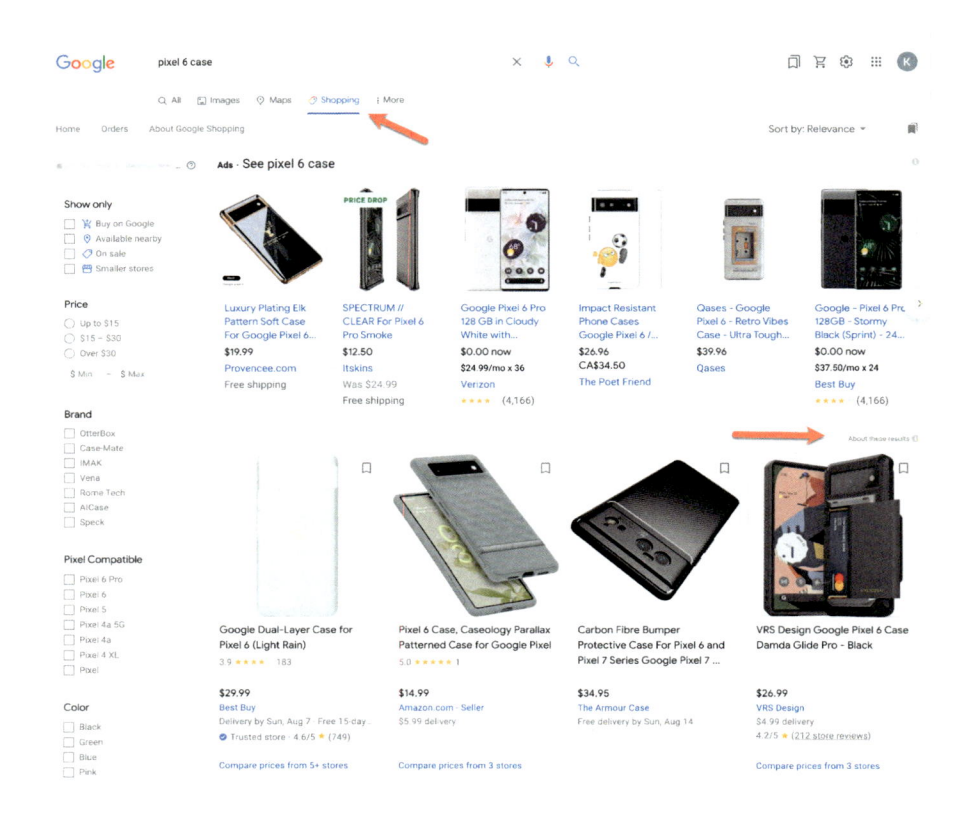

Look at the screenshot above. This is the shopping tab noted by the arrow at the top. Below this arrow, you will see the first line of products. These are paid listings, as Google would want to place the paid listings first.

Below the first line of products, you'll see the second arrow pointing to "About these results." Below are the free listings. Google will mix in some paid listings further down. Google is always testing different iterations of ad formats so the way products are presented can vary quite a bit.

Don't forget, free listings will also show in Google images, Google search, and on YouTube.

To get started with free listings:

1. Log in to your GMC account.

2. Opt-in by selecting "growth" in the left sidebar navigation and clicking "manage programs."

3. From there, click "get started" below free product listings and complete all the steps that apply to you.

This process will only take a few minutes, and once it's complete, you'll be able to start listing your products on GMC for free. So, why wait? Log in or create an account now and get started taking advantage of this great opportunity.

Shopping Ads Set Up

You can sign up for Shopping ads by clicking on the "Growth" tab in the left navigation menu of your Merchant Center account. Then, under the "Manage programs" heading, select "Shopping ads" from the list of available programs.

You can stop and start setup at any point; however, once you've started setup, Shopping ads will automatically be added to your list of pending tasks on the "Overview" page.

When you set up Shopping ads, you will need to make sure you have already added the following:

- Products

- Tax information

- Shipping

- Website verification

A Google Ads account is required to use Shopping ads. Creating or linking your Google Ads account allows product data to flow seamlessly between Google Merchant Center and Google Ads. If you're using a new Google Ads account, you'll need to set up your first campaign before linking it to your Merchant Center account. From there, you can create ad groups and add products. If you're linking an existing Google Ads account, all your current campaigns will be eligible to show Shopping ads. You can choose which ad groups and products you want to use in Shopping ads.

Linking your Google Ads account is the first step to setting up Shopping ads. Follow these steps:

1) Sign into your Merchant Center account.

2) Click the 3-dot icon in the top left corner of your screen and select Linked accounts from the drop-down menu.

3) On the Linked Accounts page, click View under "Google Ads."

4) In the "Sign in with Google" window that appears, sign in with the same Google Account that you use for your Google Ads account.

5) On the next screen, select the checkbox next to each Google Ads account that you want to link and click Done.

After you link your accounts, product data will start flowing from your Merchant Center account into your linked Google Ads account. It can take up to 24 hours for all your product data to appear in Google Ads. You can now create ad groups and add products in Google Ads.

Remember, you'll need to have at least one linked payment method before you can start running Shopping ads.

By taking these steps, you can successfully link your Google Ads and Merchant Center accounts so that product data flows seamlessly between them.

Campaign Management

After you've successfully onboarded and created a campaign, you can manage your campaign and view metrics from your Merchant Center homepage by clicking on Marketing, and then clicking Shopping ads. You can also find this information by clicking the "Campaigns" tab. From there, you can view your campaigns as well as individual ad groups and performance metrics. If you need to take action on a specific campaign or ad group, you can do so from the "Actions" column. You can also access this column by clicking on the "more" option in the campaign or ad group row. This column provides options for pausing, editing, or deleting campaigns and ad groups. Once you've made changes to a campaign or ad group, be sure to click "Save" for your changes to go into effect.

Pro Tip: While Google is trying to make it easier for you to manage everything in one place, I recommend you manage campaigns inside of the Google ads interface. There are many more features available there that you will want to take advantage of. You do not need to be a power user to work inside Google ads!

Chapter Five

GMC Products Tab

In this chapter I will be covering the Products tab which is comprised of 3 main elements.

1. Diagnostics

2. All products

3. Feeds

You will find that after you setup your account you will spend most of your time in one of these areas within the Products tab.

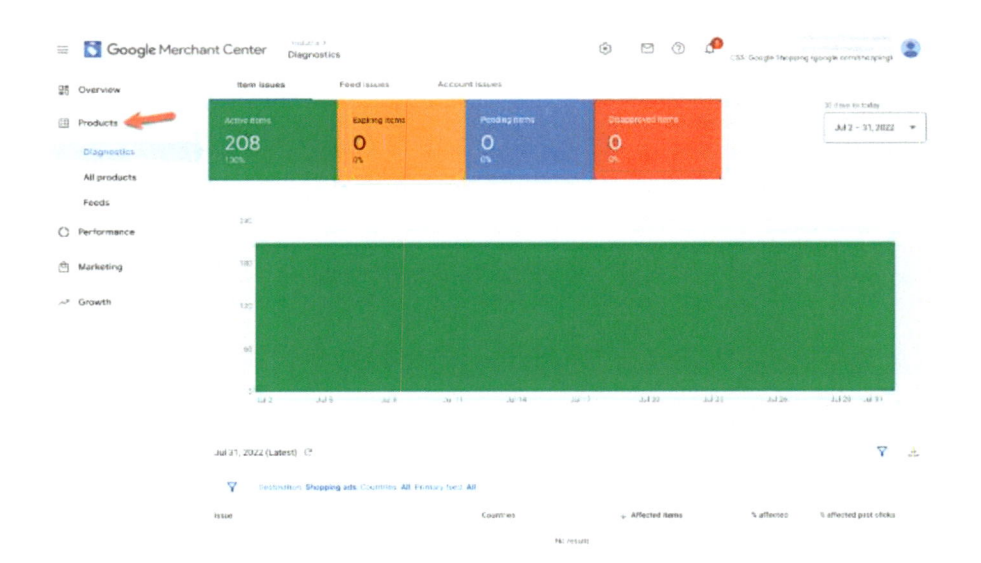

Diagnostics

Item Issues

The diagnostics section of the Google Merchant Center is a very useful tool for online retailers. It provides a summary of your product data and helps you identify any errors or problems that may exist. For example, it will show you how many products were uploaded, how many products matched the Google Shopping requirements, and how many products were disapproved.

If you have any disapproved products, the diagnostics section will tell you why they were rejected and how to fix the issue. This is extremely beneficial because it can help you avoid losing sales due to incorrect product data. You will also find that to the right of each issue a link to download the list of products that are impacted by that issue. This can be very helpful when troubleshooting.

This area is so critical to the success of your Google Shopping program that you should check each of your accounts daily for errors and changes.

I have dedicated an entire chapter to common disapprovals and how to correct them so that you can take full advantage of this powerful Google Merchant Center tool.

Feed Issues

The feed issues section of Google Merchant Center is where you troubleshoot any problems you may be having with your product data feed. This section provides a detailed list of any issues that have been found with your feed, including a description of the problem and a suggested resolution.

Simply click on the "Feed Issues" link at the top of the page to access this report. If there are any current issues, you will see a number next to the link indicating how many there are. These issues are specific to your feed, so be sure to resolve them as soon as possible to avoid any potential problems with your product listings.

Account Issues

The account issues section of Google Merchant Center is the place to start if you are having problems with your account. Towards the top of the page in the center, you will notice an account issues link. If there are issues, there will be a number next to it showing the number of current issues. Clicking on that link will take you to a page listing all the current issues with your account. From there, you can click on each issue to get more information about what is wrong and how to fix it.

In most cases, there will be a link to a help article that can walk you through the steps to fix the problem. Once you have addressed all the issues, be sure to click the "I have fixed this issue" button at the bottom of the page so that Google knows that you have taken care of everything.

> *Pro Tip:* If you are looking for an email from Google regarding account or product issues you can check in the message archive (envelope icon at top of the page) for all correspondence sent out regarding the account.

Active Items

The active items section of Google Merchant Center are products that have been successfully uploaded and matched the Google Shopping requirements. This means that these products can be seen in Google Shopping searches. To ensure your products appear in this section, you will need to make sure that all product information is accurate and up to date.

Expiring Items

Expiring items are products that will stop being shown in the Google Shopping results after a certain amount of time. This can happen if the product is no longer available or if the price expires. If you have any expiring items, the diagnostics section will tell you when they expire and how to renew them.

Pro tip: if you notice that products are expiring and you update your feed regularly, this may mean that whatever method you are uploading your product file to Google Merchant Center is failing. Products should not expire if you upload the feed daily. Typically, a product will stay on Google Shopping for 30 days without an update. At that time, the product will expire.

Pending Items

Pending items are products that have been uploaded, but Google has not yet checked them to see if they meet the Shopping requirements. If you have any pending items, the diagnostics section will tell you how many there are. and when they will be checked.

All products

The all products section of Google Merchant Center contains a list of all the products in your Merchant Center account, for different destinations.

At the top of the page, you will notice four areas that provide different information about your products. In each of the areas, if you click on the number, this will filter the products pertaining to that section.

- All products—this shows the total number of products submitted.

- Product updates—this section shows the number of new products in the last 24 hours and how many products were updated.

- Products with fix suggestions—Google not only provides suggestions for fixing product issues but also the capability of making the change right next to the product. For example, if you have a missing or incorrect global trade item number (GTIN), by clicking on the "view fix suggestion" link Google will provide an area to enter in the GTIN. This will then be applied to the feed.

- Product badges—Google is always looking for ways to help businesses be successful online. This feature automatically shows retailers when their products are eligible for badges. This update makes it easier for retailers to take advantage of the various badges that are available, including those for sale prices, price drops, and percentage off. In addition, the badges for buy quantity discounts and free shipping will now be more prominently displayed. This change will help shoppers quickly identify which products are eligible for special offers, making it more likely that they will make a purchase. For retailers, this is a valuable way to promote sales and specials and should result in an increase in traffic and conversions.

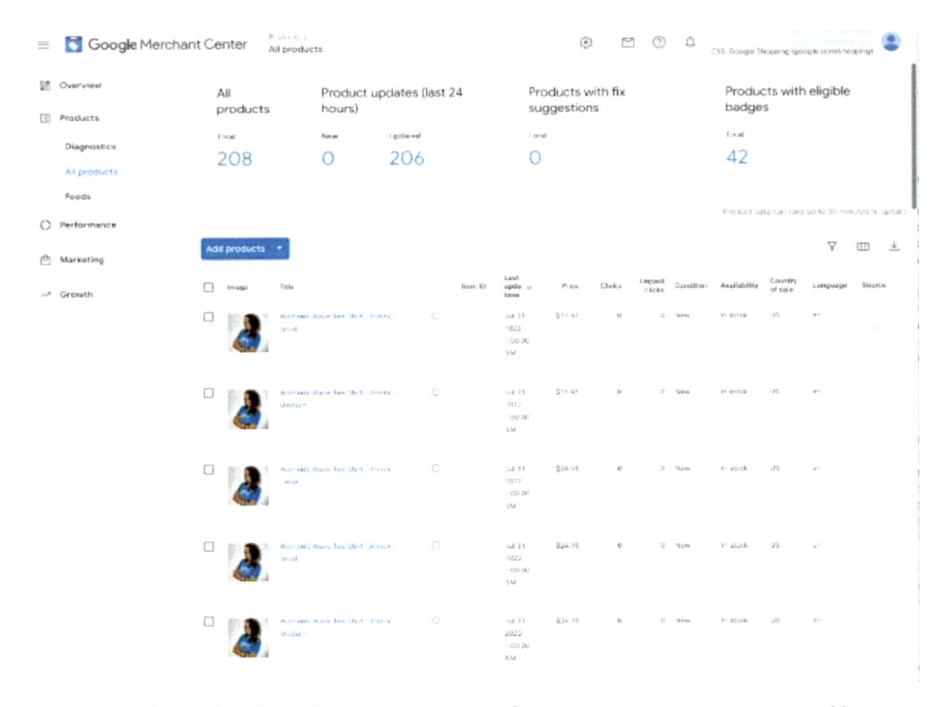

Further down the all products page is an area for managing your inventory and keeping your product information up to date. You can use this section to edit product information, add new products, or delete products.

If you are uploading products from an external source, I would recommend making product changes on the platform that sends the feed. Trying to add or delete products in the merchant center while using a product data feed will cause a lot of unnecessary confusion. Stick with one method to add and delete products.

You can also filter your products based on various feed parameters. I use this feature quite a bit when looking for a specific product or troubleshooting feed issues.

Each product title is a link that will open all the information found about that product. This is an excellent area to troubleshoot issues. Once you have clicked on the product title, there are several sections within, but I will list only the ones I feel you should be aware of.

The first has the product image and title along with the ID, price, description, etc. It also shows the eligibility status for shopping ads, dynamic remarketing, and free listings.

The next section has the technical details showing the expiration and creation dates as well as the feed name.

The regional attributes preview shows you the shipping, tax, and availability for that product for a specific location in the United States (the default is always New York, NY)

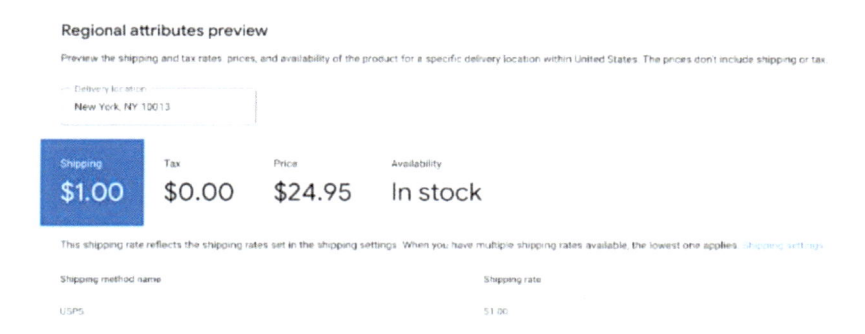

Regional attributes preview

Preview the shipping and tax rates, prices, and availability of the product for a specific delivery location within United States. The prices don't include shipping or tax.

Delivery location: New York, NY 10013

Shipping	Tax	Price	Availability
$1.00	$0.00	$24.95	In stock

This shipping rate reflects the shipping rates set in the shipping settings. When you have multiple shipping rates available, the lowest one applies. shipping settings

Shipping method name	Shipping rate
USPS	$1.00

Pro Tip: By changing the delivery location you can check to see if shipping and taxes are being applied correctly. This is especially helpful when troubleshooting an issue where Google will usually provide a zip code if it is tax or shipping related. Below is the same product but shows an area where tax is collected.

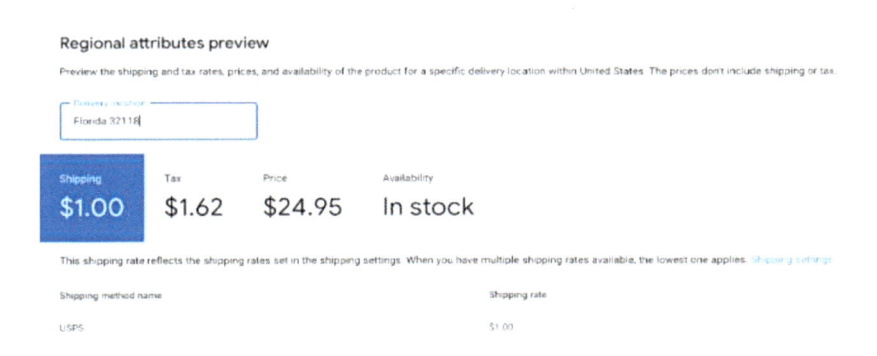

Regional attributes preview

Preview the shipping and tax rates, prices, and availability of the product for a specific delivery location within United States. The prices don't include shipping or tax.

Delivery location: Florida 32118

Shipping	Tax	Price	Availability
$1.00	$1.62	$24.95	In stock

This shipping rate reflects the shipping rates set in the shipping settings. When you have multiple shipping rates available, the lowest one applies. shipping settings

Shipping method name	Shipping rate
USPS	$1.00

The final attributes area shows the final feed and all its attributes which could potentially be combining multiple feeds. For example, if you have a supplemental feed and are updating titles for optimization purposes, the updated title will reflect here. Below this area, you may see one or more feeds and their attributes as well as information that Google has found on your site.

Feeds

Primary Feeds

Google Merchant Center uses the primary feeds to display your products on Google Shopping. You can upload your product data to Merchant Center using Google Sheets, text (.txt) files, zipped files (.gz, .zip), XML (.xml) files, or the Google Content API for Shopping. Primary feeds are the most basic way to submit your product data to Merchant Center, and they are perfect for small businesses just getting started with advertising on Google.

If you are looking for a more robust solution, consider using the Google Content API for Shopping. The API allows you to programmatically upload and manage your product data, making it easy to keep your ads up to date. Ultimately, the decision of which method to use is up to you. If you are not sure where to start, try using a primary feed. It is a simple way to get your products in front of millions of potential customers.

Supplemental Feeds

A supplemental product feed is an additional data feed that contains supplementary information about your products. These feeds can be used to provide more detailed information about your products to potential customers and can also be used to improve your product listings. This supplementary information can include things like product descriptions, pricing information, and availability. Supplemental product feeds can be a useful way to provide buyers with more complete and up-to-date information about your products. They can also help to ensure that your listings are accurate and compliant with Google's standards.

I cover supplemental feeds in more detail in Chapter 10: Product Feed Optimization. Because supplemental feeds are mostly used to optimize your data, I thought it would be a more appropriate placement.

In summary, this chapter explains the Google Merchant Center products tab, and what I consider the main hub of activity. You can find information about your products for troubleshooting purposes, you can see product images, titles, prices, descriptions, and other attribute information. You can also see if a product is eligible for shopping ads, dynamic remarketing, or free listings. Additionally, you can check the technical details and regional attributes of a product. I recommend you spend some time growing comfortable with the products tab as you will be spending a lot of time here and will want to be able to quickly navigate within it.

Chapter Six

Product Feed Specifications and Formatting

What is a Product Feed and Why do You Need One?

Creating a product feed can be a bit technical, but it is not that difficult once you understand the nuances. In this chapter, I will walk you through the components of a product feed and show you how to submit it to Google Merchant Center. I will also provide some tips on optimizing your product feed, so that you can get the most out of your listings.

A product feed is a data file that contains information about the products sold on an eCommerce website. The product feed is sometimes used to populate the product pages on the website, as well as to generate product search results. The product feed may also be used to generate product ads for display on other websites. The latter is what this book focuses on.

A product feed is a data file that contains information about the products you sell. This file is used to populate product listings or ads on Google Shopping and other shopping engines. The file can be in either XML or CSV format and must include certain required fields for each product. The product feed is typically created and managed by the merchant, although some platforms (such as Shopify) offer tools to help with this.

Think of a product data feed as a spreadsheet. The column headers in your spreadsheet will be the same as the fields that are required for each product in your store. Each row is a unique product, and each column is a piece of information about that product called an attribute.

You might be wondering "Why do I need a product feed?" The answer is simple: without a product feed, your products will not appear on Google Shopping or other shopping engines. It is the easiest way you can give information to Google about your products. If you want to sell your products online, you need to have a product feed.

Now that you know what a product feed is, let us take a look at some of the benefits:

- It allows you to get your products listed in a variety of online directories and marketplaces. This can give you a lot of exposure and help you to reach a larger audience.

- It makes it easy for potential customers to find your products. If someone is searching for a specific product, they are likely to come across your listing if you have a product feed. Product ads (Shopping Ads) feature an image along with some text about the product, and customers tend to be more drawn to this type of ad.

- Your products can be purchased just as easily as the products of the largest retailers in the world, leveling the playing field. Pretty amazing, right?

- A product feed can save you a lot of time. If you were to try and list your products in all the different directories and marketplaces manually, it would take a long time. Not to mention how long it would take to find each product and manually change the price on different marketplaces. With a product feed, you can automate the submission of your information to all these places with just a few clicks.

As you can see, there are several benefits to using a product feed. If you are not currently using one, it is something you should consider. It can save you a lot of time and help you reach a larger audience.

How to Format Your Product Data for Feeds

If you want to create or improve your product feed, then you need to format your product data correctly. This guide will show you how to do that. I will cover the basics of what a product feed is, and then I will go into more detail about how to format each piece of information. Finally, I will give some tips on troubleshooting common problems.

What are the Required Fields for a Google Product Feed?

To successfully submit your products to Google, a product feed must include certain required fields for each product. There are also optional fields that Google can use. Google loves data. The more relevant data you can provide about your product, the better!

Below are the most important fields for Google's product feed.

Required for All Products

Id (id)—A unique identifier for the product. This is typically the SKU. Making sure you have a unique value for each product is key to making it easy for the customer and yourself. Using your SKU where possible will help them find what they are looking, while keeping things tidy in databases means less clutter from inaccurate data entry or over-enthusiastic typing by staff members.

> *Pro Optimization Tip:* never change the ID for the product. Once you have decided on the ID you will need to keep it. Google uses the ID to identify the product and all its history will be attached to that ID. If you were to change the ID, you would lose all relevant history. You would basically be starting over.

Title (title)—The product name. This is the most important field after the id as it is what the customer will see first. Make sure it accurately and concisely describes the product and closely matches your website title. This is a good place to list variant attributes such as color and/or size.

It is okay to test some differences in the title. For example, on your website you might have a title of "Retro Sofa," but you might test "Retro Love Seat Couch" because loveseat and couch could have higher search volume yet still accurately describe the sofa. A note of caution here. You neither want to mislead customers, nor use excessive keywords (spam). Google will disallow products if they feel that you are misrepresenting them.

> *Pro Optimization Tip:* Frontload the most important information in the title. That is because Google only shows the first 25 characters in an ad especially on mobile, so you want that information to show first.

> *Pro Optimization Tip:* Add the brand name to the end of the product title. There is no point in using it in the front section unless it is a very popular brand. Keep in mind that the brand of the store is displayed in the ad so if you are the brand, it will already be showing on the ad. If the brand name is long, definitely add it to the end of the title. The only time I keep the brand in the beginning is if the retailer is trying to promote brand recognition or if it is popular. I generally advise against this though.

> *Pro Optimization Tip:* Do not add color to the title. People can see the color in the image of the ad. Additionally, Google is very good at referencing the color from the color field when there is a specific search query for color.

Description (description)—Here is where you use an in-depth description of the product. Highlight any unique features and benefits. Be as descriptive as possible while still maintaining good grammar and punctuation. It is OK to use formatting such as lists or italics to format your description. It is also helpful to add instructions, such as care and use of the product. You can also add how the product can be used or how it should not be used here.

Again, do not try to add excessive keywords. That will only serve to irritate customers who can see right through it. Besides, Google will penalize you for "keyword stuffing." Also, do not add promotional text or non-relevant information.

Pro Optimization Tip: Lastly, if you do not have a product description (which, strangely enough, occurs fairly frequently), add the title here. This will at least fill in the description and get your product live. You can always come back later and build out a more robust description.

Link (link)—This is the URL of the product page on your website. Make sure it is accurate and goes to the right page. If you have multiple versions of a product, such as different colors or sizes, make sure each has its own unique URL.

Image link (image_link)—This is where you will add a URL to an image of the product. The image should be high quality and accurately represent the product. This is not the place for marketing images or stock photos. The customer wants to see what they are buying so make sure the image is of the actual product.

If you have multiple images of a product, such as different angles or views, make sure each has its own unique URL.

Google prefers a white background or at the very least a light background to display the product. Make sure there is no text on the image. If the product is, for example, a box of cereal with text on it, that is okay, but Google may end up flagging the product for text and you will need to request a manual review to get the product live.

JPEG is the preferred format with PNG and BMP and TIFF also allowed. The image size should be at minimum 100 x 100 pixels for non-apparel products and 250 x 250 product pixels for apparel.

Pro Optimization Tip: Ideally you want to have at least an 800 x 800 pixel image. In Google's auction, where you are competing against others for product visibility, if all things are equal, the higher resolution image will win the auction.

Have you wondered why you need such high-resolution images? Many people think that it is because of viewing on a desktop but in actuality it is for mobile devices. Mobile devices now offer such high-resolution screens that reviewing low resolution images is a very poor user experience. Again, go with the highest resolution image you can produce.

Availability—The availability field is used to indicate whether a product is in stock. The value should be either "in stock" or "out of stock." You may also use "preorder" or "backorder" but if either of these is used, you must also add an availability date field. It is very common to find data that does not match Google accepted values. This field always needs careful attention to ensure quality and correctness.

Price (price)—This is the price of the product. To complete the price field, you will need to add the price of the product followed by the currency. For example, if the product is priced at $10 USD, you would add "10 USD" to the price field. If the product is priced in Euros, you would add "10 EUR" to the price field.

The US and Canada do not include tax in the price. For all other countries include the value added tax (VAT) or goods and service tax in the price.

For items purchased in bulk, do not submit the individual price of the item. This will be rejected. Submit the total price of the minimum purchasable quantity. For example, if you must buy 10 items to get the $1.95 a piece price, submit $19.50 as the purchase price.

Brand (brand)—This is the company that manufactures the product. The brand name of the product is important because it helps customers identify the product and manufacturer. Make sure the brand name is accurate and spelled correctly. If you are selling products from multiple brands, make sure each product has its own unique brand name. Do not put "various" or "multiple" in the brand field. This will be rejected. Also, **do not** use your store name as the brand name unless you manufacture the product.

For products that do not have a brand leave this field empty. Do not submit n/a, no brand, etc.

GTIN (gtin)—Global Trade Item Number. The GTIN is a unique identifier for a product. In the United States the most common type of GTIN is the UPC (Universal Product Code). Typically, it is the bar code found on the product packaging.

Google uses the GTIN to improve user experience and to unify products. Have you ever done a search on Google for a product and found that several retailers are listed together for that product? Google matches these retailers together under this one product with the GTIN. This is why Google is so fanatical about providing the correct GTIN. If you cannot provide this unique identifier, at the very least provide the brand and manufacturer part number (MPN). If other retailers are selling this product and you try to sell it without the GTIN, most likely your product will not rank well in the search results, if at all. If you are the only seller with this product, the product most likely will show in the search results.

A common question I heard while on the Google Shopping team was if Google knows the GTIN, why can't they provide the correct one for us? The answer was Google does not want the liability of providing an incorrect piece of data that could impact the sale of your product. Sometimes identical products have different GTINs. An example would be the manufacturer of an Acme Blue Widgetizer has one GTIN but when a popular electronics store carries the same product, it might be packaged slightly differently and given a unique GTIN. While this may not be a common use case, nevertheless, Google does not want to expose themselves to any type of liability.

MPN (mpn)—Manufacturer Part Number. The MPN is the unique alphanumeric identifier that is assigned to a product by the manufacturer. An MPN is required for all products that do not have a GTIN. There is an exception for custom made products that would not have an assigned MPN.

Condition (condition)—This is a required field if your product is used or refurbished. I generally add "new" as a default for all products unless of course they are used or refurbished.

Required for Apparel

Age group (age_group)—The target age group for the product. Allowed values: newborn, infant, toddler, kids, adult. This is another field that suffers from a lot of abuse. You would be amazed at the different content that can be placed in the age group field. In the optimization chapter I describe ways to fix common issues.

Gender (gender)—The gender for which the product is intended. As of this writing the allowed values are: male, female, unisex.

Color (color)—The color of the product. GMC supports multiple colors per product. Do not combine colors, for example, "GarnetGold." When in doubt, list the primary color found on the product. Google no longer wants "multicolor" as a value. While the color field is obviously important and will help show up in some search results unifying with other similar colors, the color in the image should be obvious when someone sees the listing. That is why I do not commonly add color to the title any longer. Google's algorithm is very good at examining an image and extracting and attributing the colors correctly for the product on the back end. They will not populate the color field with what they extract but it will help with the search results.

Size (size)—The size of the product. This attribute supports multiple sizes per product. If your products are offered in size options, it is better to send the specific size value. If a product is "One Size Fits All," or does not have a separate size field, then you may use "one_size". There are many accepted values such as S, M, L or "18/34 Tall". This field has always been one of the least restrictive regarding requirements. That said, typically issues occur when the formatting is incorrect.

Item group ID (item_group_id)—Required for product variants. This field is used to specify a common item ID for products that come in different variations like color and size. By sharing the same item ID, you indicate to Google that the products are related.

Material (material)—The material used to make the product. Some common values for material are:

- Wood
- Glass
- Stone
- Copper
- Plastic
- Rubber
- Metal
- Fabric

The material field is not as commonly used as some of the other fields but can be helpful in certain situations. For example, if you sell jewelry made from different materials, specifying the material in the product feed can help your products show up in relevant search results.

> *Pro Optimization Tip*: For products made up of multiple materials, add the primary material followed by up to two secondary materials separated by a /. For example, cotton/polyester/rayon.

Pattern (pattern)—The pattern on the product. Some common values for pattern are:

- Floral
- Geometric

- Striped

- Polka Dot

- Paisley

- Checked

As with the material field, the pattern field is not as commonly used as some of the other fields but can be helpful in certain situations. For example, if you sell shirts with different patterns, specifying the pattern in the product feed can help your products show up when a customer is searching for a shirt with that specific pattern.

Optional Product Data Fields

The following fields are optional but are highly suggested. Remember, Google loves data and many of these fields are there for Google to better understand your product.

Product type (product_type)—This is typically the category or categorization used on your website.

> *Pro Optimization Tip:* This is probably the single most important field that is not required. This is your opportunity to give Google additional information about the product. Remember when I said that Google loves data? Here is an excellent spot to give the type of data that Google loves.

The information found in the product type field is searchable! While a consumer never sees the data you place in this field, when doing a search the product type data can trigger your ad to show in the search results. As always, you do not want to insert spam keywords into this field.

Here is an example of a product type: Apparel > Dress > Mini Dress > Floral Print

> *Pro Optimization Tip*: Do not be afraid to test different variations of the above. Keep in mind that the first product type value can be used to segment your products to organize bidding and reporting in Google ads. If you make frequent changes to the first value this may negatively affect your segmentation and reporting.

Short title (short_title)—This attribute is used by Google in situations where the regular title would be truncated where Google would have a smaller display area. By using this field, you have the option to choose what to include in your title when it is abbreviated. Google recommends 5 – 65 characters despite having a 150 character limit.

> Pro Optimization Tip: Make sure to use the product name (or a product noun if the name is not clear) first, then add the brand if it is recognizable and there is room.

Additional image link (additional_image_link)—A URL to an additional image of the product.

This is an optional field but if you have additional images of the product, such as different angles or views, you can add them here. As with the initial image_link, each additional image should have its own unique URL. This is a good place to put lifestyle images, staging, graphics, or illustrations. You may submit up to ten additional product images.

Sale price (sale_price)—Only use this field if you are selling your product at a price below the normal price. Make sure that the sale price matches the landing page and the price when checking out. Do not use this field if you have a sale for 15% off and it is only applied at the checkout when using a code. You must match the price on the landing page!

To get the sale price annotation to show on your product listing, in addition to the above, the sale must be greater than five percent and less than 90%. You can check if any of your products have annotations by going into the Products tab in Google Merchant Center, then go to All Products, and apply a filter on the table choosing "Sale badge > Yes".

> *Pro Optimization Tip:* Do not populate this field with the regular price!

Google will only use the sale price for 30 days maximum. This is to prevent abuse of this feature. Once the 30-day period is over, your ads will display the regular price even if you still have a legitimate sale still in progress.

Identifier exists (identifier_exists)—The purpose of this field is to indicate if there is a unique product identifier such as GTIN, MPN, and brand available for the product. If you choose not to use this field Google assumes that the default value is yes.

If the product has a unique product identifier use yes in the field. Do not put no just because you cannot find or do not think that there is a unique product identifier. If Google believes this product has a unique product identifier your item will be flagged and will most likely have limited exposure or availability until you fix it.

Google product category (google_product_category)—pick only one category making sure it is the most relevant one. If you are unsure, move up one node in the category tree.

> *Pro Optimization Tip:* Let Google pick the correct product category. Almost always the category is correct, and it saves you a lot of time and aggravation. It does not hurt to check the categories Google picks, but I think you will rarely find mistakes.

How to Create a Product Feed in Shopify

Creating a product feed in Shopify is simple and can be done in just a few steps:

1. Login to your Shopify admin and go to Products > All products.

2. Select the export type you want from the dropdown menu. For this example, I will use the "Products (CSV for Excel)" export type.

3. Click on the Export button and wait for the file to generate. Once it is done, you can click on the Download button to download the file to your computer.

4. Open the file in a text editor or spreadsheet program, such as Microsoft Excel.

5. Make any changes or additions to the product information in the file.

6. Save the file and upload it to the platform you want to list your products on. For example, if you want to list your products on Google Shopping, you will need to upload the file in the Feeds section of Google Merchant Center.

That's it! By following these simple steps, you can create a product feed for your Shopify store quickly and easily.

An alternate method to create a product feed in Shopify is to use the Google app in Shopify and connecting it to your Google Merchant Center account. This will allow Shopify to automatically update your product information and make it easy to submit your products to Google Shopping. Additionally, there are third-party plugins available that offer different features.

To use Shopify's built-in tool, follow these steps:

1. Log in to your Shopify account and go to the Admin section.

2. In the left-hand menu, select Apps.

3. In the search bar, type in "Google Shopping" and press enter.

4. Select the app from the results and click Install app.

5. Follow the on-screen instructions to connect your Shopify store to your Google Merchant Center account.

6. Once you have connected your accounts, you can start creating your product feed.

7. To do this, go to the Products tab and select the products you want to include in your feed.

8. Once you have selected all the products you want to include, click Export to Google Shopping.

9. This will generate a file that you can submit to Google Shopping.

Third-Party Shopify Plugins

There are several third-party plugins available for Google Shopping. Some of these include:

- AdNabu

- ShopMaster

- DataFeedWatch

- Feedonomics

- GoDataFeed

Each of these plugins offers different features, so be sure to compare them before choosing one for your store. Additionally, some of these plugins may charge a monthly fee, so be sure to check the pricing before deciding on a plugin. By using a third-party plugin, you can easily create a product feed for your Shopify store.

When choosing an app, I would recommend finding one that allows you to make some changes to the feed within the app. While I do not expect an app to do everything, it may save you a lot of time later.

Chapter Seven

Methods to Create a Product Feed

Creating a product feed is an essential part of online marketing. A product feed provides Google, Microsoft Ads (Bing), or other platforms with the information they need to list your products on their websites.

To create a product feed, you first need to gather the required information. The fields required are covered in detail in the previous chapter. Once you have gathered all the required information, choose one of the following methods to generate your product feed.

Create a Product Feed in Excel

Microsoft Excel is one of the most popular tools for creating product feeds. To create a product feed, as mentioned above, you first need to gather the required information.

You can manually enter the information into the different rows and columns of the spreadsheet or sometimes you can export this information into a different type of file. If you can do the latter, choose a CSV format for the export. Most of your work will be done for you now. You may now open the file in Microsoft Excel.

Pro Optimization Tip: Make sure when you are finished editing the CSV feed that you save the file in the same format. You may get warnings from Excel to change the format to XLS or XLSM (Excel's preferred formatting), but you want to keep the CSV formatting. Google and most other feed platforms will not accept Microsoft Excel's formatting.

If you are creating the feed from scratch, you may use the following steps:

1. Open Microsoft Excel on your computer.

2. Create a new spreadsheet by clicking on the "File" menu and selecting "New."

3. Enter the required information into the spreadsheet.

4. Save the spreadsheet as a CSV file. To do this, click on the "File" menu and select "Save As." In the "Save as type" drop-down menu, select "CSV (Comma delimited)." Similar to what I mentioned above, do not get persuaded by Microsoft to use alternate formats!

5. That's it! You have now created a product feed that can be used by retailers.

Pro Optimization Tip: Make sure to check your GTIN field for correct formatting. Typically, the number will be changed to scientific notation. To remove this incorrect format or prevent this from happening, format your cells (the GTIN column) with "text" formatting. It is better to do this before adding your GTIN values because it will preserve the original formatting.

The other thing to watch for is that the leading zeros are not stripped from the GTIN, for example, 00012345678905 becomes 12345678905. Frequently, Excel will think this is a number and remove the zeros at the beginning of the number. Changing the formatting to "text" should prevent these issues!

Use Google Sheets to Create a Product Feed

Google Sheets is another popular tool for creating product feeds.

A big advantage to this program is that it can connect directly to the Google Merchant Center once finished or even prior to setup.

> *Pro Optimization Tip*: Create the Google sheet from within Google Merchant Center as described below. It will already be connected, and Google will provide you with a feed template with the column headers already filled in for you.

Anytime you want to make a change to the feed you just make it in the Google sheet and the change will be reflected in Merchant Center and directly in your ads. Of course, you need to be careful because any mistake will also directly impact your ads, but this is really the same issue for any method you choose to create a feed.

Login to Google Merchant Center (as described in Chapter 2)

Go to Products > Feeds and then click on the plus symbol in the blue circle

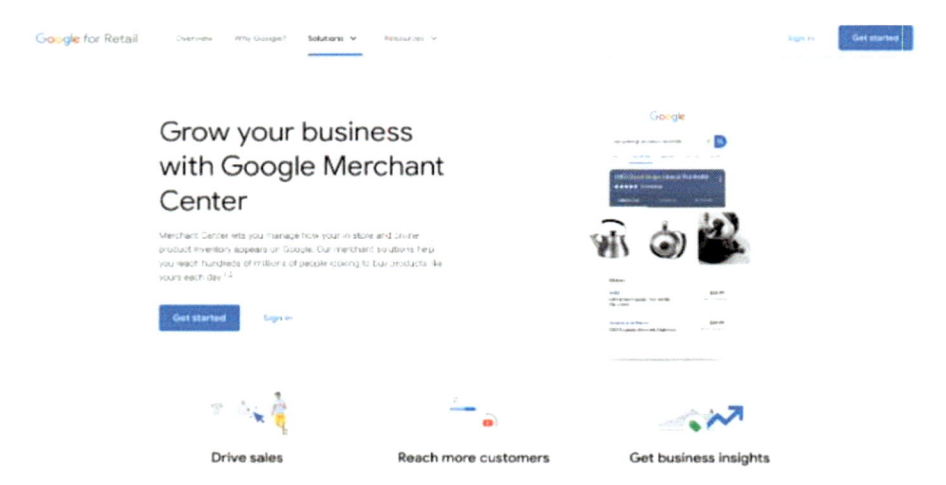

Choose Google Sheets as your Primary Feed. You can name the feed as you wish.

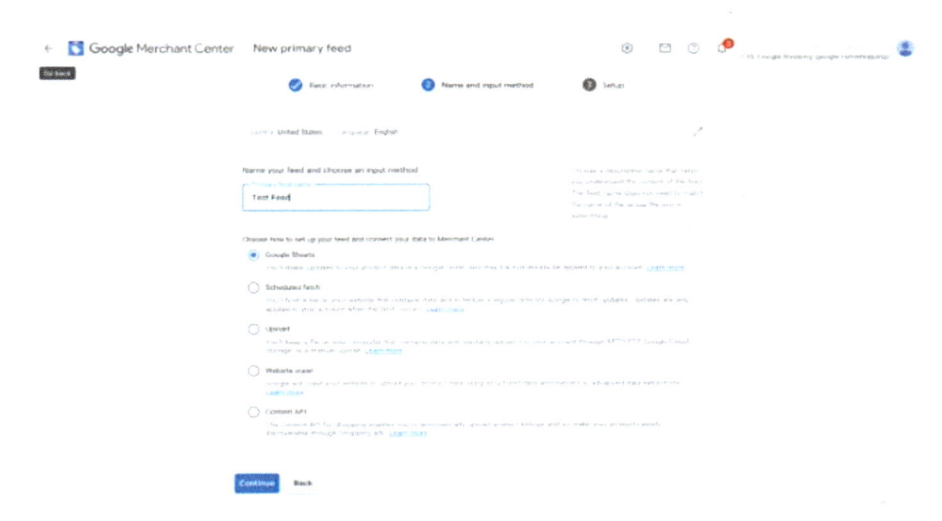

Under Setup, select Generate a new Google spreadsheet from a template.

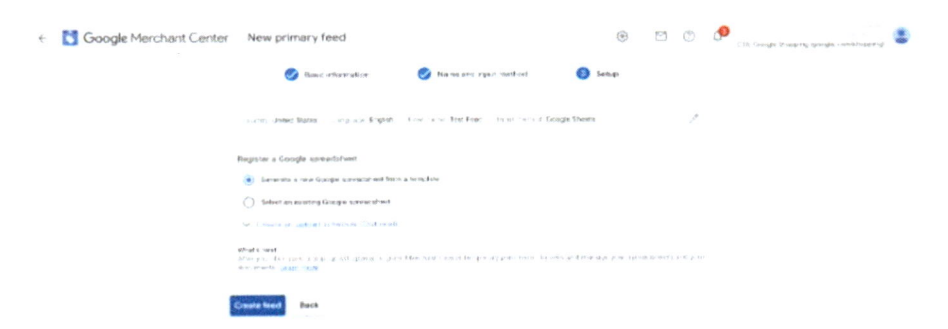

You should now have a feed created with no products. Find the link to your Google Sheet under the primary feeds. You should see "Open" which is the link to your new feed.

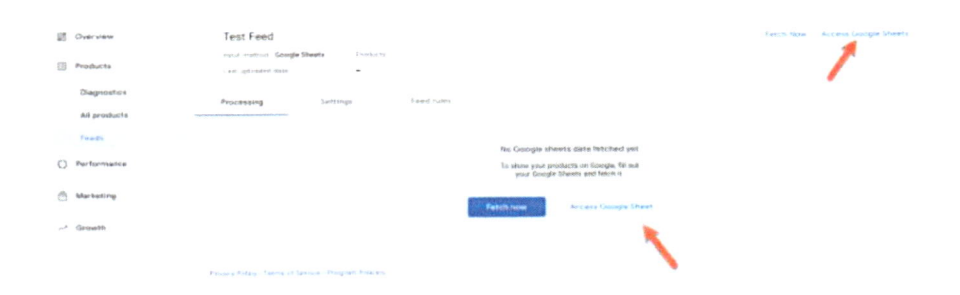

The first row should be the column header

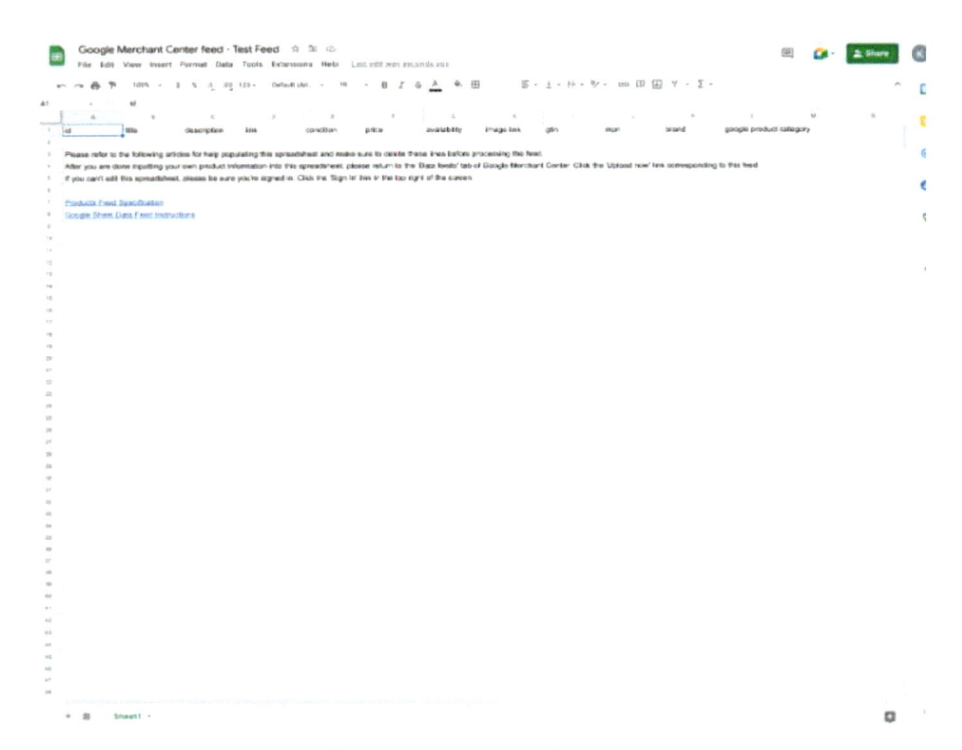

In the second row, you will enter your first product and its attributes that match the column header above. For example, in the 2nd row column one you would enter the id; in the end row column 2 you would enter the product's title, etc.

Repeat these steps for each product that you want to include in your feed.

When you are finished adding information for all your products, you have now created a product feed using Google Sheets.

Go back to your feeds list and click on the name of the file.

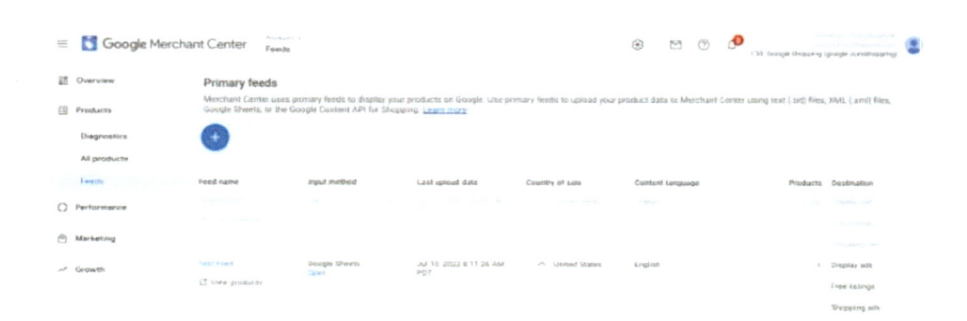

FEED YOUR BUSINESS

You must now set the schedule for the feed before going live.

> *Pro Optimization Tip*: When you set up the feed schedule make sure that the time is after scheduled updates for your website. For example, if you update the prices every evening at 11 p.m. then set your schedule to run at midnight. It is a good idea to give ample time for the data to replicate on your website before having Google pick up the feed or you deliver the feed.

I recommend you have Google pick up the feed from a URL created on the backend of your website. That is the simplest method and usually there are fewer issues.

Do not manually upload your data feeds as your main method of updating Google Merchant Center. Things will get in the way, or you will forget, and your feed will not get updated. For most merchants, one feed update a day is sufficient.

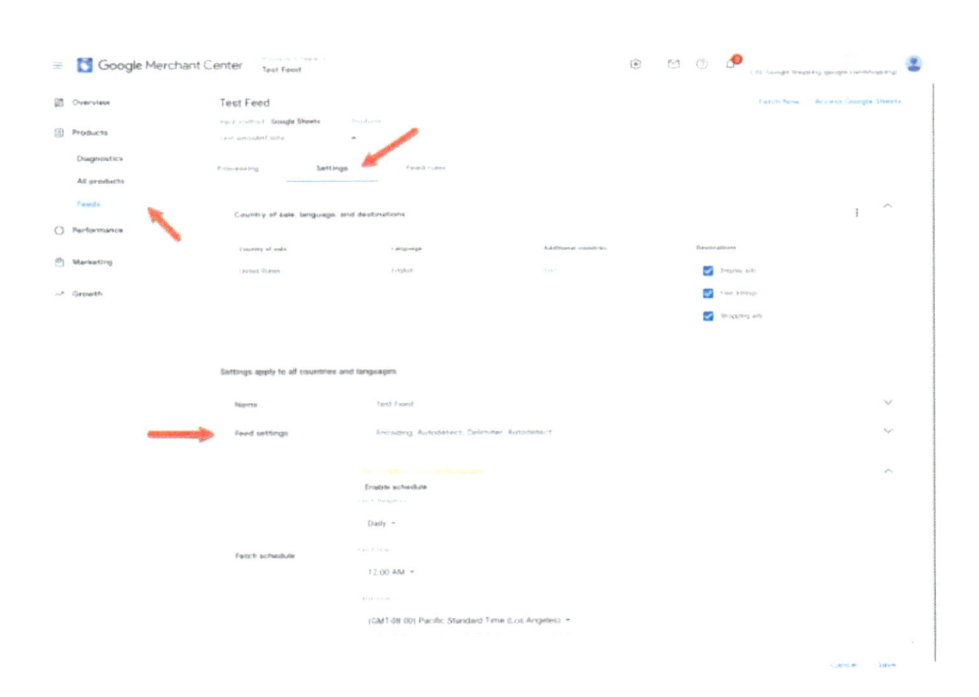

Use Third-Party Apps or Vendors to Create a Product Feed

Another way to create a product feed is to use a third-party service. These services will typically charge a fee, but they will often provide you with a more comprehensive product feed and more options to optimize your data.

These services can often be expensive, but they offer a lot of value in terms of features and data optimization. You will need to do some research to determine which one will work the best for you.

Some of the more popular choices include: GoDataFeed, DataFeedWatch, ProductsUp, and Feedonomics.

GoDataFeed.com

1. Godatafeed.com offers the ability to build a comprehensive product feed for most popular destinations

2. The service also offers options to optimize your data for better search engine visibility.

3. Godatafeed.com provides 24/7 customer support in case you need assistance setting up your product feed.

4. The service is easy to use and can be set up in minutes.

5. Godatafeed.com offers a flexible pricing plan that fits most budgets.

Datafeedwatch.com

1. Datafeedwatch offers a wide range of features, including the ability to create customized rules to optimize your data.

2. The service is easy to use, with a user-friendly interface. They offer support but the quickest response time is during the day in Europe due to their location

3. Datafeedwatch offers a Shopify app that makes importing data very easy. My only complaint (at the time of writing) is the lack of integration with a supplemental feed within the Datafeedwatch portal. You can work around this with a supplemental feed within Google Merchant Center but then the data is being changed in two different portals which is less than ideal.

FEED YOUR BUSINESS

4. For the record, Datafeedwatch is my current platform of choice because of the tool itself and the pricing.

5. Datafeedwatch offers a 15-day free trial period so you can test out the service before you commit to a subscription.

ProductsUp

1. ProductsUp offers a wide variety of connectors to help you get started quickly, including support for major eCommerce platforms like Shopify, Magento, and BigCommerce.

2. ProductsUp allows you to customize your product data to optimize it for search engines and other channels.

3. ProductsUp provides detailed performance tracking so you can see how your products are performing across all channels.

4. ProductsUp offers a wide range of export options, including CSV, XML, and JSON.

5. ProductsUp has a team of experts available to help you get the most out of their service.

6. Productsup has a great tool where you can visualize and create datapoint connections.

7. Productsup is more expensive than the first two listed, so if you are a small retailer, it might not be worth the cost.

Feedonomics

1. Feedonomics is a full-service platform offering feed optimization, management, and support.

2. Feedonomics is best for retailers or agencies that do not want to manage or have a very large inventory of products. This is not a self-serve, do-it-yourself platform.

3. Feedonomics is more expensive than the others discussed here but it is a fully managed solution

Manually Input Products into a Spreadsheet or Google Merchant Center

In Google Merchant Center you can create and manage your product data. I would not recommend this method unless you have just a handful of products. If you have less that 20 products and you never update prices this may be the feed building method of choice. This is basically the same method as using Google Sheets.

- If you enter manually in Google Merchant Center, your products are automatically updated. If you create a separate spreadsheet, you need to manually upload.

- Use the Google sheet method above instead of this option!

In you insist on continuing with this method to manually create the feed you will need to do the following:

1. Go to https://merchantcenter.google.com/ and click on "Sign in."

2. Click on the "Products" tab and then click on "Feeds."

3. Click on the "plus" sign to create a new feed.

4. Enter the required information into the feed as outlined in the previous chapter.

5. Save the feed and you are finished!

It sounds simple but everything must be done manually. There are far better choices to create feeds which will save you a lot of time in the long run.

Use an API to Create a Product Feed

If you have the technical skills, an API can be used to create a product feed automatically. This is the most advanced method, but it offers the advantage of being able to include more data and meet specific requirements for various platforms and channels.

There are several ways an API can be used to create a product feed. APIs allow developers to programmatically access the catalog data and create a feed that meets the requirements of various platforms and channels.

This is a very advanced topic and requires coding to access the API and create data feeds, so I am including it for information purposes only. I recommend staying away from this format unless using a pre-built solution such as:

- Google Merchant Center API

- Shopify API

- Third-Party app

Creating a product feed can be a complex process, but there are several ways to get the job done. In this chapter, I have covered five methods for creating a product feed: manual entry, Excel/CSV import, data scraping, using an API, and using a pre-built solution. Each method has its own advantages and disadvantages depending on your needs and skill level. Whichever method you choose, make sure that the data in your product feed is accurate and up-to-date and easy for you to update.

FAQ

What are the benefits of creating a product feed?

Product feeds are a great way to provide potential customers with detailed information about your products. By having a product feed, you can make it easier for customers to find the products they are looking for and compare prices between different retailers. Additionally, product feeds can be used to generate traffic to your website or blog and increase your visibility in search engines.

What are some common mistakes when creating a product feed?

Not including all required fields, using the wrong data format, and not updating the feed regularly. Be sure to avoid these mistakes to create an effective product feed.

What format should my product feed be in?

Product feeds can be in a number of different formats, including CSV, XML, TSV, and TXT. The format you choose will depend on the platform or channel you are using to distribute your product feed. Most platforms and channels have specific requirements for the format of the product feed, so be sure to check before you build the feed. Google allows XML, TSV, and TXT.

How often should I update my product feed?

This will depend on how often your products change. Usually, one time a day is sufficient for most retailers. Remember to set up the schedule to run after products are normally updated.

What are some common product feed errors?

- Incorrect product identifiers

- Missing or incorrect images

- Incomplete or inaccurate data

- Unparsable text

Chapter 11 is dedicated to common errors and how to fix them.

Chapter Eight

Shopify's Google Channel App

More and more retailers are choosing to use Shopify as their eCommerce platform of choice. There are several reasons for this, but the three main ones are convenience, features, and customer service.

Convenience is a big factor for many retailers. Shopify makes it easy to set up an online store and manage it from one central location. They also make it easy to create a product feed and get it live on Google Merchant Center. This takes the hassle out of running an online business and lets retailers focus on what they do best: selling products.

Features are another big reason why retailers love Shopify. The platform offers a wide range of features that let businesses customize their stores to match their specific needs. This includes everything from inventory management to payment processing to shipping options and data feed management. Plus, new features are being added all the time, so retailers can always find something that meets their needs.

Customer service is the third main reason why retailers choose Shopify. It has one of the best customer support teams in the industry, with experts who are always available to help businesses get started and solve any problems they encounter along the way. Plus, there are lots of helpful resources available online, such as video tutorials and user guides, so retailers can always find answers to their questions quickly and easily.

Shopify has also made it easy to market your products. One of the apps developed by the Shopify team is the Google Channel app. The app automatically syncs your products and information about your Shopify store with the Google Merchant Center. You can then update your Google product listings directly from your Shopify store.

Shopify stores selling in the United States using Shopify's Google channel can now appear in the Google Shopping tab listings for free. You can also create paid Shopping campaigns for better visibility.

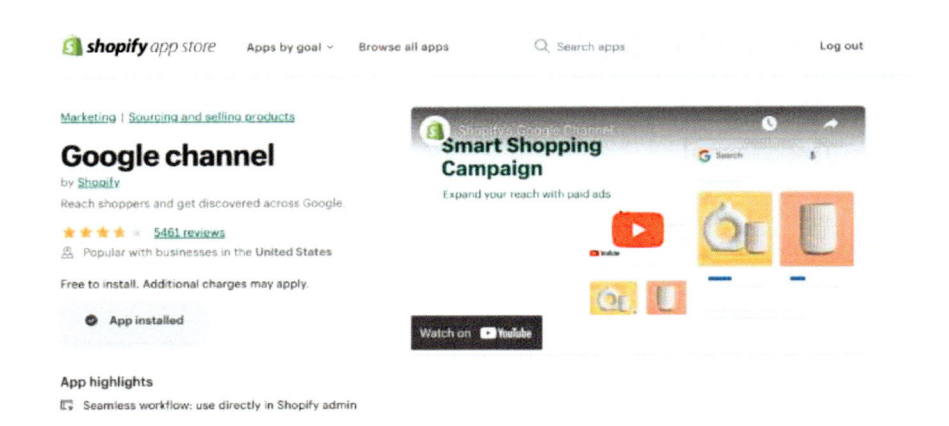

How do you get the Shopify Google channel app?

To get the Shopify Google channel app:

1. Log in to your Shopify account.

2. Go to the Shopify App Store.

3. Search for "Google Shopping" and select the "Google Shopping" app.

4. Add channel.

5. Next you will connect your Google account by selecting an existing account or creating a new one. You will need to allow Shopify access to your Google account.

6. Review the setup requirements for your online store (covered in a previous chapter).

7. Select or create a merchant center account (described in a previous chapter).

8. Verify yourself as the Merchant Center account owner using phone verification.

9. Select the target market, currency, and language for your products.

10. If you will use paid advertising on Google, select shipping settings and either automatically import or manually set up the settings.

Pro Optimization Tip: When you are syncing products to Google Shopping, you have the option to sync your product titles and descriptions or use the title tag and meta description from the search engine listing. In most cases, it is helpful to use the search engine listing title tag and meta description so that you can include more keywords for search engine optimization (SEO) on Google Shopping. This way, you can optimize your product listings on Google Shopping without changing the product information in your online store.

Keep in mind that the title tag and meta description from the search engine listing may not be perfectly optimized for your products, but it is a good starting point. You can always tweak the title tag and meta description as needed or create a supplemental feed for optimization (more on this in Chapter 10).

Should you use the Shopify Google Channel App?

Pros:

1. It is one of the quickest and easiest ways to get your products listed on Google shopping.

2. The Shopify app connects via the API; therefore, products are updated quickly.

3. The app is free! There is no charge to install and use daily. If you are okay with adding a supplemental feed or feed rules, both found in Google Merchant Center, then you have a no-cost solution for selling your products on Google.

Cons:

1. The product ID is different than what you use in your Shopify store. Typically, the product ID is your SKU but Shopify formats the id as "Shopify_(CountryID)_XXX_YYYY. This can create problems such as setting up your remarketing tags which would usually use the ID (SKU) on your website. You must customize your remarketing tags to synchronize with the Shopify IDs if you use the app. Keep in mind that once you have sent your feed to Google, the ID should not be changed later down the road. Changing the product ID removes the product performance history and is like adding a brand-new product and starting over. Additionally, you may have trouble matching a Shopify ID to your store IDs when it comes to reporting and troubleshooting. It adds another step to have to match these.

2. Feed optimization is next to impossible without setting up a supplemental feed or using feed rules in Google Merchant Center. You can try using the page title tags and meta descriptions, but they may not get you the desired results

3. The app can be slow and "buggy" if you have a lot of products.

My Recommendations

If you are looking for simplicity and your feed has ample data, and is optimized, then go with the app. But it is rare that I see all the above! Most likely you will need to add or change data, so the choice is between whether to do it on the front end, that is before it goes to Merchant Center, or on the back end, after it is in Merchant Center.

Also, if you decide to use the app you will need to make changes to the Google Ads' remarketing code to match your product ID. The remarketing code will want to use your Shopify store ID which will be different than the Shopify Google Channel app ID.

Ultimately, when it comes to using the Shopify Google Channel app, there is no right or wrong answer—it depends on your specific needs and goals.

Troubleshooting

If you are finding errors in the app it is often due to certain required attributes not being filled in. Go to the "editing" section of the app where you can make changes to the products in bulk.

The first attribute I would check is the custom product. If you have GTINs then you want the custom product to be set to false. If there are no GTINs then it should be true. Check the other required attributes to make sure they are all filled in. For example. I have an apparel retailer where the age group, gender, and condition are usually blank and need to be set manually.

Chapter Nine

Submitting Your Feed

Now that you have completed your product feed, it is time to submit it to Google Merchant Center. You can do this by logging into your Merchant Center account and going to the "Products" tab. From there, you will see an "Add a product" button. Click on this and then select "Submit a data feed." Choose the file that you want to submit and click "Upload." Your product feed will now be sent to Google for processing.

It is important to note that you will need to resubmit your product feed any time that you make changes to it. This includes adding or removing products, changing prices, or changing any of the other attributes in your feed. Failure to resubmit your feed after making changes could result in your products being removed from Google Shopping.

So that was painless, right? Well, hold on. Do you really want to upload feeds manually every time you make a change to the website? Will you really remember each time? Would you be happier if you could automate the process? Absolutely!

FTP

Standing for File Transfer Protocol, FTP is a network protocol used to transfer files from one computer to another. By using FTP, you can automatically upload your product feed to Google Merchant Center each time it is updated. This means that you do not have to remember to do it manually and you can be sure that your feed is always up to date.

There are a few things that you need to set up to use FTP for your product feed. First, you will need an FTP client. This is a software program that allows you to connect to an FTP server. There are many different FTP clients available, both free and paid. Some popular ones include FileZilla, SmartFTP, and CuteFTP.

Next, you will need the address of an FTP server. This is the computer that will host your product feed file. You can either use a public FTP server or set up your own private server. If you choose to use a public server, make sure that it is reliable and has enough storage space for your product feed.

Finally, you will need the login details for the FTP server. This includes the server address, username, and password. Once you have all this information, you are ready to set up FTP for your product feed.

To start, open your FTP client and connect to the FTP server. Then, navigate to the directory where you want to upload your product feed file. Once you are in the correct directory, simply drag and drop your file into the window. Your product feed will now be uploaded to the FTP server and Google Merchant Center.

If you ever need to make changes to your product feed, simply update the file on your computer and upload it again using FTP. This way, you can be sure that your product information is always up-to-date and accurate.

What are the Steps to Create FTP in Google Merchant Center?

There are two ways to submit your data feed to Google Merchant Center: via FTP or through the Content API for Shopping.

To set up an FTP account:

1. Log into your Google Merchant Center account.

2. Click on the "Tools" Icon at the top of the page and choose SFTP/FTP/GCS

3. Choose either SFTP settings or FTP settings

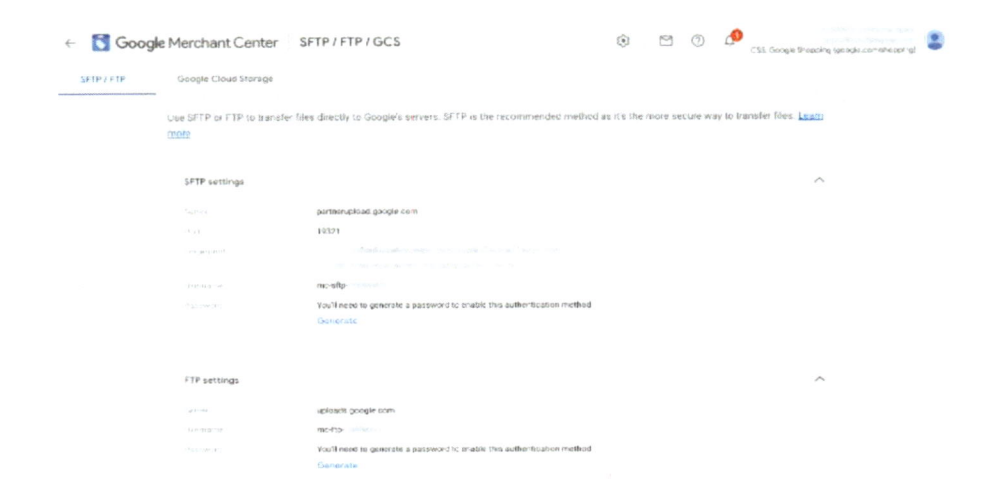

1. Your FTP server hostname will be ftp.google.com and your username will be "mc-sftp-" of mc-ftp-"your Merchant Center ID followed by (e.g., if your Merchant Center ID is 12345, your username will be mc-sftp-12345).

2. Next, click "generate link" which will create a unique password. Your FTP account password will be generated and displayed on the screen. Make sure to copy and save this password in a secure location, as you will not be able to retrieve it later.

3. You are now ready to upload your data feed file to the FTP server. To do this, you will need an FTP client such as FileZilla or WS_FTP.

4. Once you have logged into the FTP server, you will need to navigate to the /public_html/ directory.

5. In the /public_html/ directory, you will need to create a new directory for your data feed files. This directory can be named anything you like (e.g., "myfeeds").

6. Upload your data feed file(s) into this new directory.

7. Once the upload is complete, you will need to log into your Merchant Center account and navigate to the "Products >Feeds" section (found in left navigation bar)

8. Click on the "+" button under Primary Feeds

9. Pick the country and language. Enter a name for your data feed and select "Upload.

10. In the "File name" field, enter the name of your data feed file (e.g., myfeed.xml).

11. Once you have entered all the required information, click on the "Create feed" button.

Pro Tip: Click on (Upload a file now (optional). You can now upload a file as a test by checking off the upload as test box. I highly recommend doing this before uploading your feet for production. You will find out if there are any errors at this time and then you can correct them before going live.

You have now successfully submitted your data feed to Google Merchant Center!

Go Fetch

You can also set up FTP for your product feed and provide the URL of where the file is located to Google Merchant Center. Google will then "fetch" the file from the URL that you provide on a regular basis. This means that you do not have to upload the file each time that you make a change, as Google will do it for you.

To set up fetch, login to your Merchant Center account and go to the "Products" tab. From there, click on the "Add a product" button and select "Submit a data feed." Choose the option for "I'll upload my own file by FTP" and enter the URL of your product feed file. Then, click on the "Save & Continue" button. Your product feed will now be fetched by Google on a regular basis.

If you ever need to make changes to your product feed, simply update the file at the URL that you provided, and Google will fetch the new file the next time that it checks. This is a great way to keep your product information up to date without having to do any work.

What if I use Google Sheets?

If you use Google Sheets to manage your product information, you can set up Google Merchant Center to fetch your product feed automatically. To do this, go to the "Products" tab in your Merchant Center account and click on the "Add a product" button. Then, select "Fetch a data feed."

On the next page, enter the URL of your product feed into the "File URL" field. You can find this URL by going to File > Publish to the web in Google Sheets. Then, select "Web page" from the "Link" drop-down menu and copy the link that is provided.

Next, choose how often you want Google Merchant Center to fetch your product feed. The options are hourly, daily, or weekly. Finally, click on the "Fetch Now & Schedule" button. Your product feed will now be fetched automatically from Google Sheets.

API

What if I have several thousand products and make frequent changes?

If you have many products and make frequent changes to your product information, it might not be practical to use FTP or fetch. In this case, you can investigate delivering the feed via the API. This is a more advanced option that requires some development work, but it can be worth it if you have a lot of products and need to make changes often.

The API will update products in Google Merchant Center as soon as the changes are made. This means that you do not have to worry about scheduling. As soon as you make a change to your product information, it will be updated in Google Merchant Center.

If you are looking for a solution that offers an API connection, I recommend that you check out third-party vendors. They can help you get started with the API and make sure that your product information is quickly up to date.

A few choices include:

- DataFeedWatch

- ProductsUp

- GoDataFeed

- Feedonomics

No matter which option you choose, make sure that you select a reputable company that can offer quality customer support. This way, you can be sure that you are getting the most out of your product feed and keeping your product information up to date as well as getting help when you need it.

Now that you know how to submit your product feed, it is time to choose the method that works best for you. FTP is a great option if you want to have control over the file and make changes as needed. Google Sheets works well if you do not have too many products, and you set up Google Merchant Center to fetch your product feed automatically. The API, great for very large feeds or for frequently changing products, will update products in Google Merchant Center as soon as the changes are made. This means that you do not need to be concerned about scheduling or anything like that. As soon as you make a change to your product information, it will be updated in Google Merchant Center.

Chapter Ten

Product Feed Optimization

What is Product Feed Optimization?

Product feed optimization is a process of making sure your product data is complete, accurate, and formatted correctly for Google Shopping. By doing this, you can improve your chances of appearing in front of potential customers at the moment they are searching for what you offer. A fully optimized feed helps Google determine when to show your ads and where. The more relevant your product is to a user's search, the more likely your product will show. Optimizing your product feed can be time-consuming, but it is worth it in the end. Not only will you be more visible to potential customers, but you will also save money on advertising costs. And of course, that can lead to more clicks, more sales, and a healthier bottom line.

Product feed optimization is also the process of improving the quality and effectiveness of a product data feed. While it is important that the data is properly formatted and that all required information is included, there is more to this story. Just as importantly, the data must be accurate and up-to-date, relevant to the customer's needs, and descriptive enough to drive conversions. In short, product feed optimization is about making sure that every element of a company's product data is working together to maximum effect. When done correctly, it can be a powerful tool for driving sales and growth.

Before you optimize your entire feed, start with a small test group of products. This will allow you to make changes quickly and easily without affecting too many products.

Second, clearly define your goals for the optimization test. What are you hoping to achieve? This will help you determine what success looks like. Finally, be patient. Results from tests can take time to come in, so do not give up too soon. If you keep these tips in mind, you will be well on your way to optimizing your product feed for success. I provide additional information on testing later in this chapter under A/B Testing.

Identify and Correct Errors in your Data

When identifying errors in your data, it is important to first understand the types of errors that can occur. There are three main types of errors: omission, commission, and incorrect information.

Omission errors occur when important information is left out of the data feed. This can result in a loss of potential sales, as Google may not show your ad for a product that is not included in your feed. Commission errors, on the other hand, occur when incorrect information is included in the data. This can lead to mismatches between what you offer and what Google thinks you are selling, which can cause your ads to be disapproved or ranked lower than they should be. Finally, incorrect information can also lead to lost sales, as customers may not be able to find what they are looking for on your site.

To correct these errors, it is important to first identify where they are occurring. You can do this by reviewing your data feed and comparing it to your online store. Once you have identified the errors, you can then correct them by adding missing information or fixing incorrect values. It is also important to keep your data up to date, as changes (such as inventory levels or prices) can cause discrepancies if they are not updated regularly.

Add Keywords to your Product Title

There are a few reasons why you might want to add keywords to your product title. The first is that it can help your product show up in more search results. This is because the keywords will be used by Google when indexing your product listings. The second is that it can help improve your click-through rate (CTR). This is because your listing will be more relevant to the customer's search query, and therefore more likely to be clicked on. The third is that it can help you rank higher in search results. This is because Google considers the relevance of your listing when determining its position in the search results. By including keywords in your product title, you are making your listing more relevant to the customer's search query, which can help you rank higher.

Choose the Right Keywords for your Products

When it comes to choosing keywords for your products, there are a few things to keep in mind. First, you want to make sure that the keywords are relevant to your product. This means that they should be specific enough to target what you are selling, but also general enough so that they will be used by many people.

Second, you want to make sure that the keywords are included in your data feed. This can be done by adding them as keywords or product titles, or by using them in your product descriptions. You want to make sure that the keywords are used correctly. This means using them in the correct order and including them in the correct fields.

> *Pro Optimization Tip:* Be careful when applying keywords to the title. You do not want to change the title so much that Google disallows the product because the title does not match the landing page. Always test a small number of products first before applying the optimization to the broader feed. That way if there are any issues, you can catch them early on.

> *Pro Optimization Tip:* When it comes to keyword usage, you want to make sure that you are not stuffing the title or description with too many keywords. This can result in your ad being disapproved or your product ranking lower than it should. Instead, focus on using a few relevant keywords in the title or the description so that it flows naturally.

There are a few different ways that you can find keywords for your products. The first way is to use keyword research tools, such as Google AdWords, Keyword Planner, or a third-party tool like Moz Keyword Explorer. These tools will allow you to see how often people are searching for certain keywords, as well as what the competition is like for those keywords.

Another way to find keywords is to look at your competitor's product listings and ads. This can give you an idea of what keywords they are using for their products.

You can also use your product data to find relevant keywords. This can be done by looking at the title and description fields in your data feed. By understanding how these fields are used, you can identify which keywords are most likely to be used by potential customers.

Finally, review the search terms report generated in your Shopping campaigns in Google Ads. These are the actual search terms that customers are using to find your products. Make sure you have the conversions column added and filter from high to low. Obviously, you want to look closely at the search terms that are generating conversions. Determine if you should add these to the title, description, or product type. Don't be spammy about it. Only use these words if they add additional relevant context to the product offering.

Product Category Title Optimization

What category your product falls under will affect how you should optimize your product title. The following are some general guidelines to follow. Also review Chapter 6: Product Feed Specifications for additional information.

Apparel

Brand + Gender + Product Type + Attributes (size, color, material).

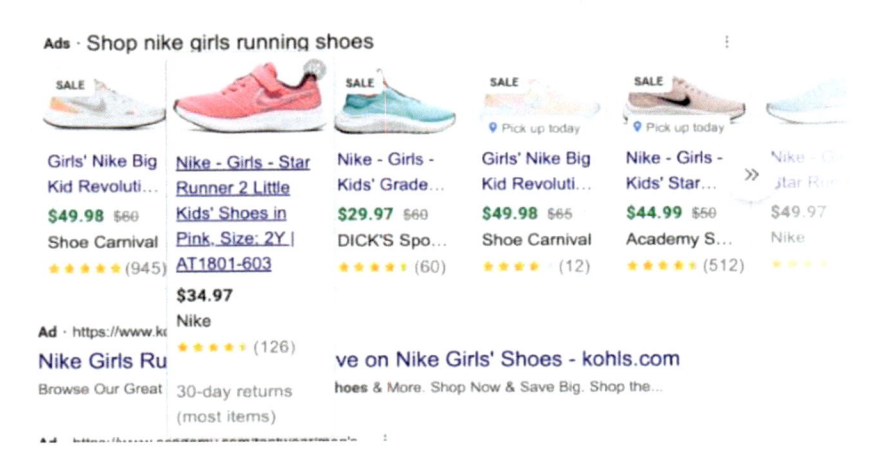

Electronics

Brand +Attributes + Product Type + Model Number

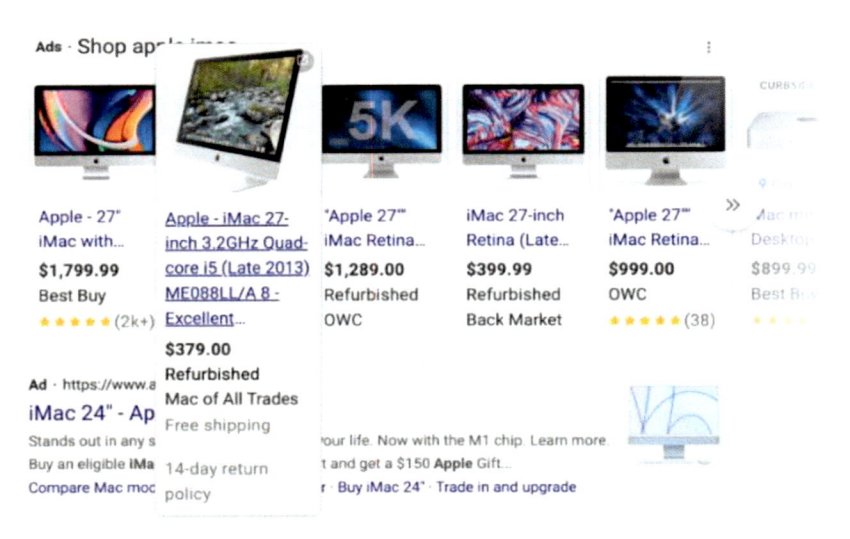

Consumables

Brand + Product Type + Attributes (weight, count)

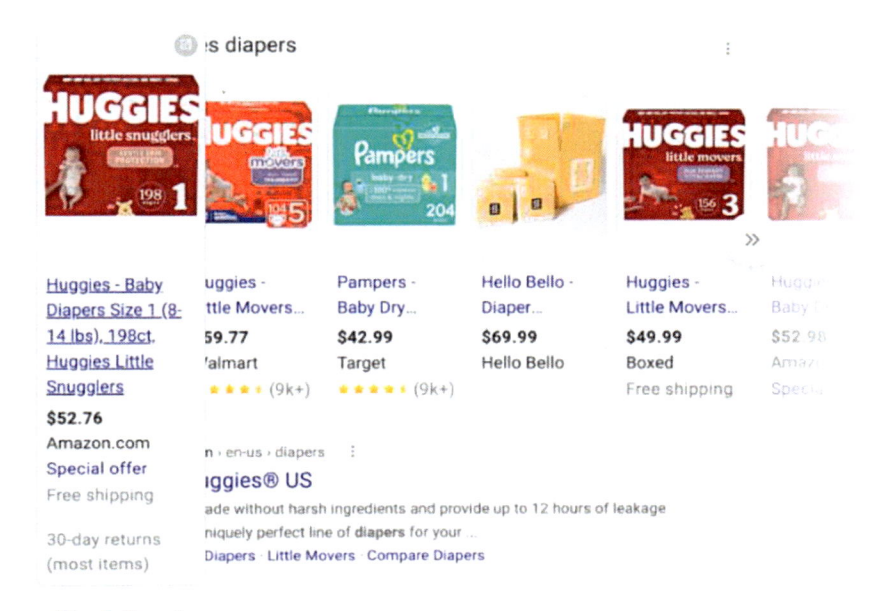

Hard Goods

Brand + Product + Attributes (quantity, color, size, weight)

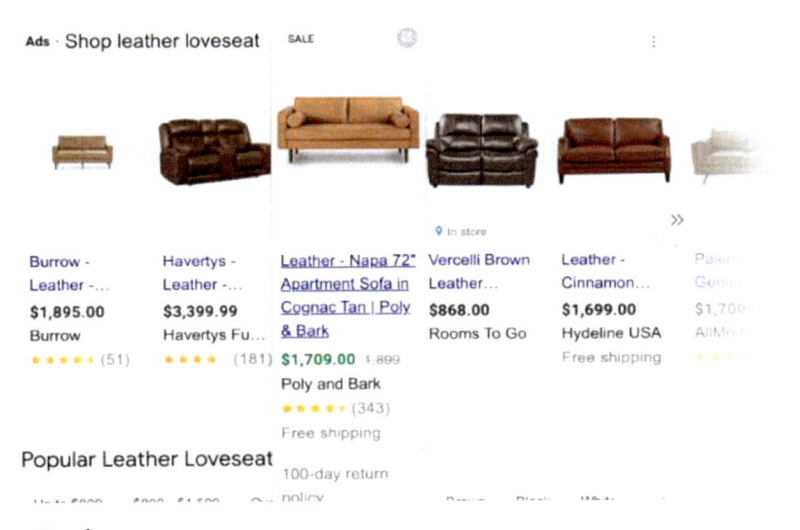

Books

Title + Type + Format + Author

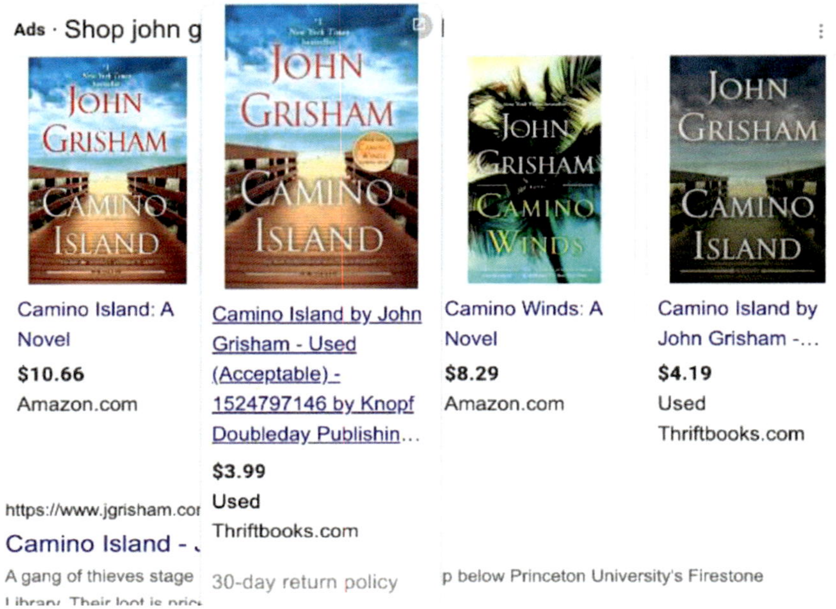

Seasonal

Occasion + Product Type + Attributes

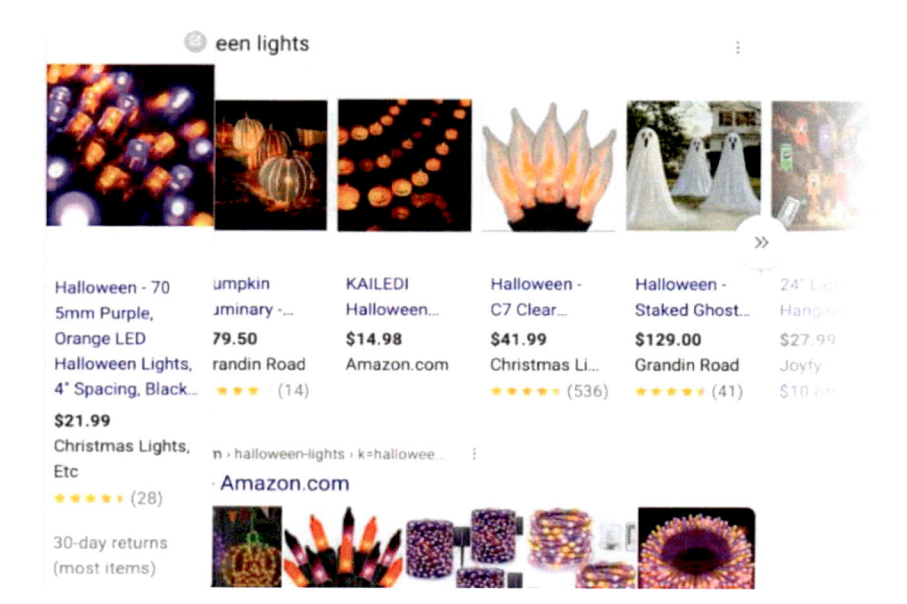

Keep in mind that there is no hard and fast rule to follow. These guidelines are offered as suggestions and usually produce good results when used correctly.

How To Optimize your Product Descriptions

When it comes to optimizing your product descriptions, there are a few things to remember. First, you want to make sure that the description is accurate and up to date. This means including all relevant information about the product, such as its features, benefits, and specifications. Second, you want to make sure that the description is clear and concise. This means using simple language that can be easily understood by potential customers. Some say written content should be at the fifth grade level for best results. Finally, you want to make sure that the description is keyword rich. This means including relevant keywords throughout the description so that they can be easily found by potential customers.

Supplemental Feeds

What is a Supplemental Product Feed?

A supplemental product feed is an additional data feed that contains supplementary information about your products. You might be wondering why I would include this in the optimization section? Because almost always a supplemental feed is used to enhance or optimize your existing product data.

A supplemental product feed can be used to provide additional product details, such as product variations, pricing changes, and new product offerings. This type of feed can also be used to correct errors in your primary feed or to provide updated product information in a timely manner.

In general, supplemental feeds are a valuable tool for any merchant who wants to maintain a high degree of control over their product listings. However, it is important to note that supplemental feeds come with their own set of rules and guidelines.

How do I Set Up a Supplemental Feed?

Setting up a supplemental feed for your website is a relatively simple process that can be easily completed using Google Merchant Center.

1. Log into your Google Merchant Center account.
2. In the left menu bar, select Products > Feeds.
3. Click on the blue Add supplemental feed under Supplemental feeds.

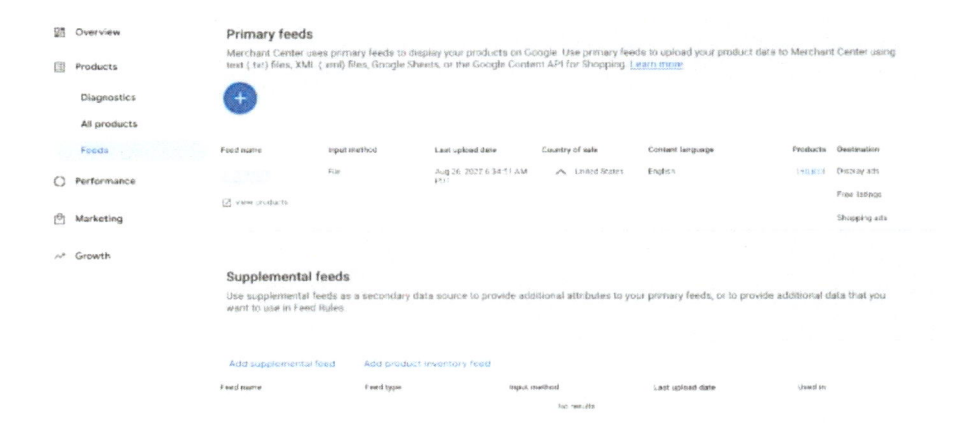

4. Enter a name for your supplemental product feed and select Google Sheets then click Continue.

5. You now need to register a Google Sheet. You can choose to generate a new spreadsheet from a template or select an existing Google Sheet. You can also set up the schedule to run the supplemental feed in the same window. I would recommend a daily schedule, slightly after the time you run your primary feed.

6. When setting up the supplemental feed you need to start with the ID. This needs to be the same ID as what is used in the primary feed. This joins the two feeds together. It is how Google knows to match and join the data together. The ID is the only required attribute when using a supplemental feed. Keep in mind, that this will override existing data if you are not careful!

7. You can now add whatever columns you want and corresponding data within. Below are examples that I often use.

Examples of How to Use a Supplemental Feed

Adding GTINs

If you obtain a missing GTIN or one that can be used to correct a bad GTIN, add a GTIN column (make sure it is identical spelling and capitalization as the primary feed). Add the product ID in the ID column and the corresponding GTIN. When you run the supplemental feed, you will now have added the new or updated GTIN value to your product listing in Google Merchant Center.

Adding Promotions to a Specific Group of Products.

When creating a promotion for a limited number of products you typically will want to use the promotion_id attribute which is an optional attribute in the product feed. To set this up, provide a list of products in the ID column and then add the promotion to the promotion_id column. The value you add is not seen by customers. I usually use something that is relevant to the promotion. For example, for Black Friday in 2022, I would use BF2022 but of course you can use anything that makes sense to you.

When you set up the promotion in Google Merchant Center, you will tell Google to apply the promotion only to products with this promotion ID.

Overwriting Values

For example, you can quickly change titles and test performance. Let's say you change 10 products' titles to see if this will boost sales. You need some way to measure the performance. I recommend adding a value in a custom label field indicating this is a test in addition to the title change. This gives you the ability to run a report that filters on the custom label and looks at the performance compared to the other titles.

Bid Strategies

Add custom labels that can then be used for the segmentation of bids. Some examples that could be used are breaking out your top selling products and raising the bids only on these products. You would run a report in Google Ads and filter on products that have the highest conversion value. Then, add this list of product IDs in the supplemental feed and apply a "top seller" label to the custom labels.

When you set up the product group in Google Ads, you will use this custom label to filter this group of products and then set the bids accordingly.

You could also do the same with low performing products. Add a label of "low performer" to a group of products that have high ad costs but low or no sales. Following the same steps above except you would want to lower the bids for these products.

Additional strategies could leverage products with high margins, seasonal products, price segmentation, and more.

A/B Testing

A/B testing is a method of comparing two versions of a webpage, app, or in our case change to the data feed to see which one performs better. Version A is the control, while version B is the test variant.

To run an A/B test, traffic is split evenly between the two versions so that each visitor has an equal chance of seeing either version. The goal is to find out which version leads to more conversions.

A/B testing can be used to test anything from adding a keyword to a title to changing the product image shown. By carefully designing and analyzing experiments, businesses can make data-driven decisions about how to improve their websites and apps.

Here are a few examples you might want to explore:

1. Change the product type for a group of products by adding a keyword that represents an important feature that customers search for.

2. Try testing different bid strategies for different groups of products. You can do this by adding custom labels to your product data, and then creating separate bids for products that have those labels.

3. Experiment with changing the titles of your products. This can help you understand which title variations result in the best product listing performance.

When performing A/B tests here are a few best practices to keep in mind:

1. Always test one change at a time.

2. Test changes that you think will have the biggest impact.

3. Keep track of what you are testing and how it affects your data.

4. Use a control group to help you determine whether the change had an effect.

5. Be prepared to discard changes that don't have an effect or make things worse.

Optimizing your product feed for Google Merchant Center is an important step in making sure that your products are accurately represented and can compete with or surpass your competition. By following the simple steps outlined above, you can ensure that your products will be fully optimized. Remember to be careful when using a supplemental feed, however, as it can override existing data in your primary feed. Lastly, always be testing. You should always be looking for new opportunities to exploit!

Chapter Eleven

Troubleshooting Common Product Feed Problems

Feed issues, from basic mistakes to processing errors, can have a devastating effect on your ads,. For example, a price discrepancy or incorrect availability can quickly turn potential customers away. Even something as simple as insufficient product data can be damaging, preventing customers from finding the items they need. In addition, processing errors can cause your ads to be rejected outright. As a result, it is essential to be vigilant in maintaining your feed.

I will not cover every possible policy violation. I will discuss some of the most common errors that I have encountered while creating or uploading product feeds and what I have helped my clients with. I will also provide solutions to help you fix these errors quickly and easily. So, if you are having trouble with your product feed, be sure to read this chapter carefully!

Google's Policy Violations

Merchant center accounts are reviewed on a regular basis to ensure compliance with product specification requirements. If it is found that your product data is not in compliance, you will receive a warning email with examples of the issues that need to be fixed, and a timeframe in which to fix them. Failure to fix the issues in the specified timeframe may result in your account being suspended. Therefore, it is important to take these warnings seriously and take action to correct the problems as soon as possible.

There are basically two levels of violations and warnings: data quality suspension warnings and preemptive item disapproval warnings. Data quality suspensions are where the entire account is shut down whereas the preemptive item disapproval is at the product or item level. Obviously, both will impact your bottom line, but account suspensions are the more serious of the two and should not be taken lightly.

Invalid Product IDs

Invalid product IDs are one of the most common errors that you may encounter while creating or uploading your product feed. There are a few reasons why this may happen:

- The product ID is missing from your feed.

- The product ID is invalid (e.g., it contains characters that are not numbers, letters, underscores, or dashes).

- The product ID is too long (50-character maximum limit).

To fix this problem, you will need to make sure that all your product IDs are valid as described above. You can do this by double-checking your feed to ensure that all the product IDs are present and correct. If you find any invalid product IDs, you will need to update them before you upload your feed again.

Missing Product Image URLs

Another common error that you may encounter is missing product image URLs. This can happen for a few reasons:

- The product image URL is missing from your feed.

- The product image URL is invalid (e.g., it does not begin with "http://" or "https://").

- The product image URL is too long (2000-character limit).

- It is not in one of the supported formats (JPEG, WebP, PNG, GIF, BMP, or TIFF).

- Symbols are present and need to be replaced with URL encoded entities ((&) should be replaced with %26 or (,) should be replaced with %2C).

Invalid Product Titles

Invalid product titles are another common error that you may encounter while creating or uploading your product feed. There are a few reasons why this may happen:
- The product title is missing from your feed—to fix, add a valid product title.

- The product title is invalid (e.g., it is common to see HTML code in titles). To fix, remove HTML or invalid encoded characters.

- The product title is too long (150 characters). To fix this, shorten the title to 150 characters or less.

- There are words with all letters capitalized. It is okay to have the first letter capitalized but Google looks at words with all caps as spam. Change all cap words to only the first letter capitalized.

- There is promotional text. Remove promotions to fix this issue.

Missing Product Descriptions

Missing product descriptions are another common error that you may encounter while creating or uploading your product feed. There are a few reasons why this may happen:
- The product description is missing from your feed or is too short. To fix a missing description add the product title. If it is too short, append some attributes like size, color, weight, or MPN.

- The product description is invalid (e.g., it has HTML code instead of ASCII characters). You will need to replace the invalid code with ASCII characters.

- There is promotional text. To fix this, remove the promotional text.

Incorrect Domain Submitted

The domain does not match your store domain. To fix this, make sure you are using the same domain that is verified in Google Merchant Center.

Promotional Overlay on the Image

This is where some sort of promotion is present on the image. You can remove this by opting into the Google image improvement tool and letting Google try and remove the promotion from the image. You can also explore using an alternate image that does not have the promotional overlay.

Image too Small or Low Image Quality

For example, the minimum size requirement of 100 x 100 pixels or 250 x 250 pixels for clothing is not met. The best solution is to source an image that meets the requirements. I wish I could tell you that you could just make the existing image bigger but that does not work.

Availability

Incorrect values submitted or unclear values on the website. There are only four values accepted at present. Those are in stock, out of stock, backorder, or preorder. The value needs to be one of these. You can easily apply feed rules (found in Google Merchant

Center and discussed later) or a find and replace the rule in your feed platform to make bulk changes to values that do not meet the requirements.

If you have automatic item updates active, it is possible that Google is picking up the incorrect availability from your microdata. This is not so easily identified because Google overwrites your values with what it collects (scrapes) from your website. To fix this, you would need to review the microdata and change it to the correct availability.

Price Issues

Specify currency. For example, in the US you would use USD.
 No free items are allowed to be advertised.
 Do not include tax in the price for the US and Canada. You do include tax in the price for all other countries.

Missing or Incorrect Required Attribute [price]

You have not assigned the currency (USD or appropriate for country), or it may be formatted incorrectly. It is also possible that the field is blank or is an incorrect value (non-numeric or 0).

Invalid Price Format [sale price]

Usually, a comma is used instead of a dot or there are too many decimal places.

Price Mismatch

The price in the feed needs to match what is on the website. There are a few reasons this could be happening. You may have a sale that has started, and you are not sending the sale price in the feed. Or it may be as simple as your sale price is not as obvious to Google as

Google would like. I have seen where the regular price is crossed out lightly and the sale price is in place, but Google still picked up the regular price.

Another common cause is you may have made a price change on the website since the last time a feed was processed. Therefore, it is important to have the feed process relatively close to the time that you make changes on the website.

If you are using something as sophisticated as IP detection that dynamically changes the price based on your customer's location this also could be the issue. Keep in mind that Google's support team is usually in India and what they see may be different than what your customer sees. IP detection does not play well with Google Shopping!

Sometimes there can be a problem that is less obvious. If you have outdated microdata or HTML, Google may scrape your site for pricing and pull incorrect information from this code. Keep in mind that this code is not customer-facing but Google still uses this data. You will need to look at the HTML or review the page in a tool like Google's Schema Markup Testing Tool.

Lastly, the variant pricing may not be obvious. For example, if the landing page shows one price for product A but you have a different price for the product B variant, you should have the landing page price for the product B variant displayed correctly when someone clicks on the B variant and lands on the page.

Missing Value [shipping]

This error would occur if you neglected to set up shipping in Google Merchant Center or you did not provide shipping rates for some products. This is a required attribute for every product in every country. The easiest way to fix this is in Google Merchant Center. Click the tools icon, then go to shipping and returns and click the plus sign. After that, you will fill in the necessary fields to complete the shipping information.

Missing Shipping Weight Attribute

When setting up shipping in your merchant account, rules may have been set up based on product weight. You will need to make sure the shipping_weight field is added to the feed and filled in appropriately for each product.

Inaccurate Shipping Costs

Google has found that the amount you are charging for shipping at checkout is different than what you have listed in Google Merchant Center. One thing to note, Google will only cite you when the shipping costs at checkout are greater than what is in Google Merchant Center. If you overestimate shipping in Google Merchant Center and the actual cost is less for the customer when checking out, you will not get a suspension warning. I mention this because sometimes it is impossible to determine the shipping costs for large or heavy items due to shipping via freight, so it is not unusual for retailers to overestimate the charge in Google Merchant Center.

To fix the issue, review the violation examples provided by Google and review these products by going through the purchase process and comparing your shipping prices with what is in Google Merchant Center. Apply corrections as necessary and once completed, submit for review.

Missing Value [tax]

Either tax was not set up for the account or it may be missing for a set of products. Go into merchant center, then to tools in the settings menu, select sales tax, and click the tax settings tab. Here you will add the tax information as needed. This is described earlier in the book.

Inaccurate Tax Information

Usually, this error occurs when the tax information is not set up in Google Merchant Center for a particular state. Google will supply you with examples of products and the ZIP Code where they tested the tax and it did not match the tax that you are collecting on your website. Check where the ZIP Code is in Google's examples of products with tax errors and then go into Google Merchant Center into the Tax settings and set up sales tax for that ZIP Code/state.

I recommend using Google determined sales tax which is an automatic setup. Trying to manually set up the sales tax is next to impossible. because there are often variations within counties and cities.

Limited Performance due to Missing Identifiers

This warning is because your products are missing more than one product identifier. To fix this, add the correct product identifiers for all products.

GTIN

Limited Performance due to Missing GTIN

This warning is because your products are missing the GTIN value. The solution for fixing this problem is adding a GTIN value.

Invalid GTIN

Something about the GTIN submitted is incorrect. Most likely you will need to go to your product source to verify the GTIN.

Ambiguous GTIN

Valid GTINS are usually 8, 12, 13, or 14 digits long. The most common cause is too few digits caused by leading zeros being stripped off. For example, the GTIN value of 000123456789 often is changed to 123456789 because spreadsheets like real numbers and real numbers do not have zeros at the beginning. To prevent this from happening when viewing a feed within a spreadsheet like Excel or Google Sheets, change the GTIN column formatting to text. This will keep the values unchanged. This also prevents the spreadsheet from changing the GTIN to a number with scientific notation—another common issue seen with GTINs.

Reserved GTIN

This indicates the GTIN has not been released for use by GS1 (the entity that controls GTINs) but is reserved for future use. To fix this, go to your supplier and let them know about the issue.

Restricted GTIN

Google is indicating the GTIN is invalid because it cannot have a prefix of 2, 02, or 04. These codes are restricted for special purposes. To fix this, go to your supplier and let them know about the issue.

Incorrect Value [identifier exists]

The "identifier exists" field is used to tell Google if there is a unique identifier (GTIN, Brand, MPN) for this product. The accepted values are True or False. Most likely you have entered False but Google has identified the same product is offered by other vendors with a unique identifier. To fix this, you will need to set the value to True and obtain the GTIN/Brand/MPN.

Product Identifiers Provided but identifier_exists Set to False

This indicates the identifier_exists attribute is set to false, but you have provided one or more of the product identifiers. To fix, set the identifier_exists to True.

Feed Processing errors

Incorrect Feed URL

This error occurs while submitting your product feed to Google. Usually there are additional characters in your feed URL, or the feed is in an incorrect format. To fix this, make sure your feed is either a .txt or .xml file and that there are no accidental characters or spaces added to the URL.

Items Uploaded Through Multiple Feeds (warning)

This warning occurs when the same product is submitted through more than one feed. This warning is frequently seen when switching over to a new feed while the old feed is still live. This will usually resolve quickly after removing the old feed from Merchant Center. The other reason this issue may occur is when two products mistakenly have the same ID. To fix this issue, make sure that each product has a unique ID.

Item Disapproved due to Policy Violation

This error is particularly frustrating because it does not give you any clues as to what is wrong with your feed. The only conclusion that can be drawn from the error message is that Google's algorithms have found elements in your feed (or in your online store) that are not in line with Google Shopping policies. So, what can you do if you receive this error? The first step is to review the policies that apply to your product category. Next, look for banned words in your titles and descriptions.

While Google's support used to be bad it has improved some. You can try contacting Google and requesting more information about the problem. During the conversation, make sure to ask for a case number so you can respond later and reference the case.

Do not be surprised if Google will not give you the reason for the disapproval. Google's rationale is that many are trying to game the system and after getting the reason for the disapproval you will then try and circumvent them. It can be very frustrating!

I recommend remaining calm and asking questions to probe for possible solutions. If you reach someone that is not helpful, I have found that by giving an honest review at the end of the call you will usually be contacted by a manager regarding your dissatisfaction.

You can also call again, start fresh, and potentially talk to a more helpful support person. I have had issues that have taken weeks of back and forth before getting a satisfactory solution.

Once you are certain that you are in compliance with all the relevant policies, then you can submit an appeal to Google. Be sure to include as much evidence as possible to support your case.

Unavailable Desktop or Mobile Landing Page

This error means that for some reason Google is unable to connect to the landing page. It could be a 404 error where the page is not available yet or no longer available (often due to changes made on the website) or Google could not connect (HTTP 5xx response). The easiest way to verify this is to click on the link (product page URL) and see if you connect. If you do, it is possible this will resolve on its own on the next feed update. I would also check your robots.txt file to make sure you are not blocking Google's web crawler. You can usually find this by typing in "yourdomain.com/robots.txt". Look for what is disallowed and talk to your webmaster if you have questions.

Misrepresentation

In 2020, Google updated its system to suspend online stores they feel are suspicious. You could be suspended if Google feels that you are not being truthful or accurate in how you represent your store or your products. For example, you might advertise one price, but the price is higher unless the customer makes an additional purchase of another product. If you do not clearly detail this in the promotion Google will flag this for misrepresentation.

Another misrepresentation issue that pops up is not having complete and accurate business information either on your website and/or on Google Merchant Center. To fix this issue, you will need to complete the missing information that Google has determined is an issue. Usually, you will need your business address and phone number in Google Merchant center and a valid contact method on your website.

You may have to dig into your account a bit to figure out what Google thinks is unacceptable. Counterfeit goods, adult-oriented content, and banned products are all possible reasons for a misrepresentation suspension. It does not necessarily mean you are doing this, but Google might think that you are. Most likely, if you contact Google they will not explicitly tell you what the problem is. As I stated elsewhere in this chapter, google often thinks retailers are trying to trick their systems and by giving you the answer to your problem, they think you will try and circumvent their system

In this chapter, I have discussed some of the most common errors that you may encounter while creating or uploading your product feed. I have also provided solutions to help you fix these errors quickly and easily. Google's algorithm is constantly changing, and so are Google's policies and enforcement. While I have attempted to provide the most up-to-date information, it is very possible a new set of policies has created additional enforcement warnings. So, if you are having trouble with a suspension or warning and it is not covered in this chapter, most likely, there are others experiencing the same problem. Search the web for the issue, and you probably will find some tips for handling the problem.

Chapter Twelve

Google Merchant Center Feed Rules

What are Feed Rules?

Feed rules is a tool found in Google Merchant Center that allows you to transform your data in a way that matches Google's product requirements. You can use this feed processing tool for resolving errors and optimizing your product data. Each time the feed runs, feed rules will apply changes to your feed if the criteria that you established are met.

What I really like about this tool is that you can test out the new feed rule before applying it live. Google will provide feedback after the test run to show you how the rule could potentially change the feed. If you do not like the outcome, you can remove the rule!

One thing to watch out for when applying a feed rule within Google Merchant Center is keeping track of what changes you are making. It is possible that you could be troubleshooting an issue and if you have a third-party feed platform or app where you can make changes in addition to feed rules in Google merchant center, it can be difficult to locate what and where changes are being made.

Where do I Find Feed Rules?

To find feed rules, log in to your Google Merchant Center account. On the left-hand side navigation panel, click on "Products" and then "Feeds." Find the name of the feed that you want to work on and click on the three vertical dots next to it. In the drop-down menu, select the " Feed rules." tool.

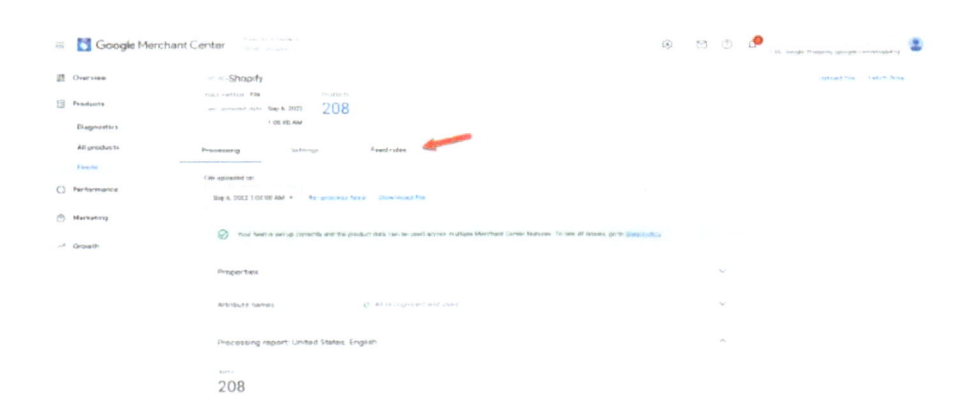

How do I Create a Rule?

To create a rule, click on the blue "+ ADD A RULE" button. This will open a side panel where you can start to build your rule.

I will start with the data source operations. You can choose from Set to, Set to multiple, Extract, or Take latest.

- "Set to" will completely replace the original data with what you specify in the next field.

- "Set to multiple" lets you specify multiple values that will be set as new data points.

- "Extract" pulls data from a specific field and places it in the new field that you specify.

- "Take latest" will keep the most recent data from fields that have multiple values.

After choosing your operation, select which field you want to apply the rule to. You can also specify if this rule is only applied to certain types of items by clicking on the "Conditions" drop down and selecting your preference.

Now it is time to specify the value that you want to set the field to. If you chose "Set to multiple," you will need to add each value on a new line.

Next is where you add the modifications. There are nine different modification operations. You can choose from Prepend, Append, Standardize, Add repeated field, Optimize URL, Find & Replace, Calculate, Split & choose, and Clear.

- "Prepend" and "Append" let you add text to the beginning or end of a field, respectively.

- "Standardize" changes the format of a field to match Google's product specification requirements.

- "Add repeated field" allows you to duplicate fields with different values.

- "Optimize URL" makes sure that your links are pointing to the right place and are clean from any excess characters.

- "Find & Replace" lets you search for specific text in a field and replace it with different text.

- "Calculate" can add, subtract, multiply, or divide fields to create a new value.

- "Split & choose" breaks up a field into multiple values which can then be placed into different fields.

- "Clear" removes all the data from a field.

After you have chosen your modification, click on the "Modify value" drop down and select what part of the field you want to modify. If you are adding multiple values, each value will need to be on a new line.

Before you submit your rule, you may want to use Conditions. Conditions are helpful if you want to make sure that a rule is only applied in certain circumstances. For example, you may want to apply a rule only to items that are in stock. To do this, click on the icon to the left of "Conditions" and specify your conditions. You can have multiple conditions and you can also choose whether all or any of the conditions need to be met.

Once you are finished, click on the "Save as draft" button to save your changes.

You will now be redirected to the main Feed rules page where you can Apply, Discard, or Test changes. I recommend testing your changes before going live. it takes a little while for the report to be generated but once completed you will have a good understanding of how the new feed rule will impact your product data feed.

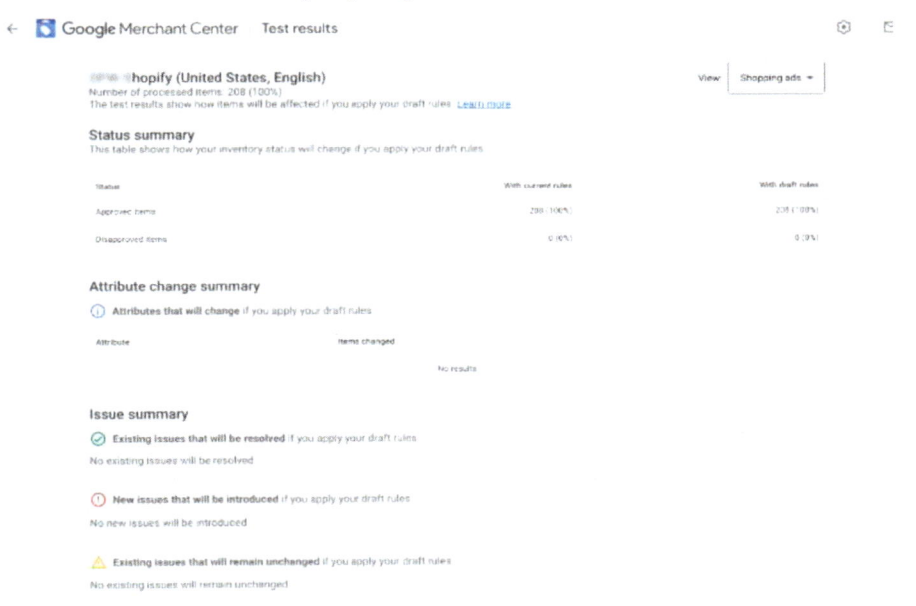

You can see in the screenshot that Google will report if any existing issues will be resolved or if any new issues were introduced. If you are satisfied with the change then apply the new rule. If not, you can discard the rule and try again!

If you want to make changes to an existing rule, click on the three vertical dots next to the rule and select "Edit." This will open the side panel so you can make changes to your rule.

You also have the option to delete a rule by clicking on the three vertical dots next to the rule and selecting "Delete."

Finally, you can disable a rule by clicking on the toggle switch next to the rule. This is helpful if you want to temporarily turn off a rule without having to delete it.

Now that you understand how to use feed rules, we can look at some real-life examples.

Feed Rules Examples

Append Brand to Title

For this example, I will append the brand to the title, but you could substitute the brand with the color or size or some other attribute.

1. Click on the blue + button.

2. Find the source that you want to edit. In this case it will be the title. This will open a new screen.

3. On the left-hand side you should see Modifications - Add modification. Click this. Now you will see the option to click on "Append."

4. This will open a box "Type or select". We want to select "primary feed: Brand". It should look like: this:

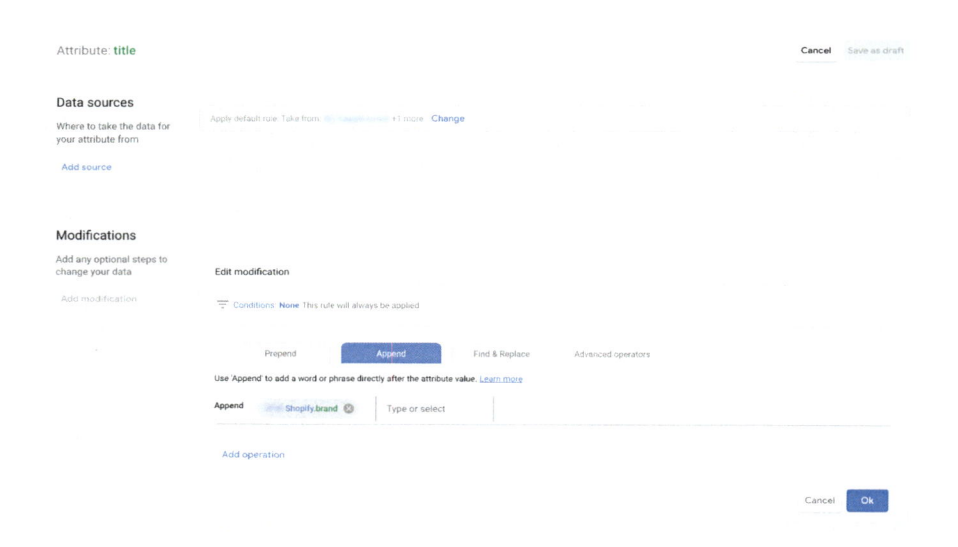

5. Click OK and then Save as draft. If you look in the column to the right you will see the Brand has no space between the title and the Brand. Let's make a quick change.

6. Open your text editor and type in a space with your space bar. Now copy that space you created.

7. Add an operation, click Append, and paste what you just copied. You should now see something like this ' '. Click on it, which lets Google know this is what you want.

8. To the right of this you will see an arrow pointing up. Clicking on this moves this rule to the top. We want the space to go first and then the Brand to be appended. It should look like this:

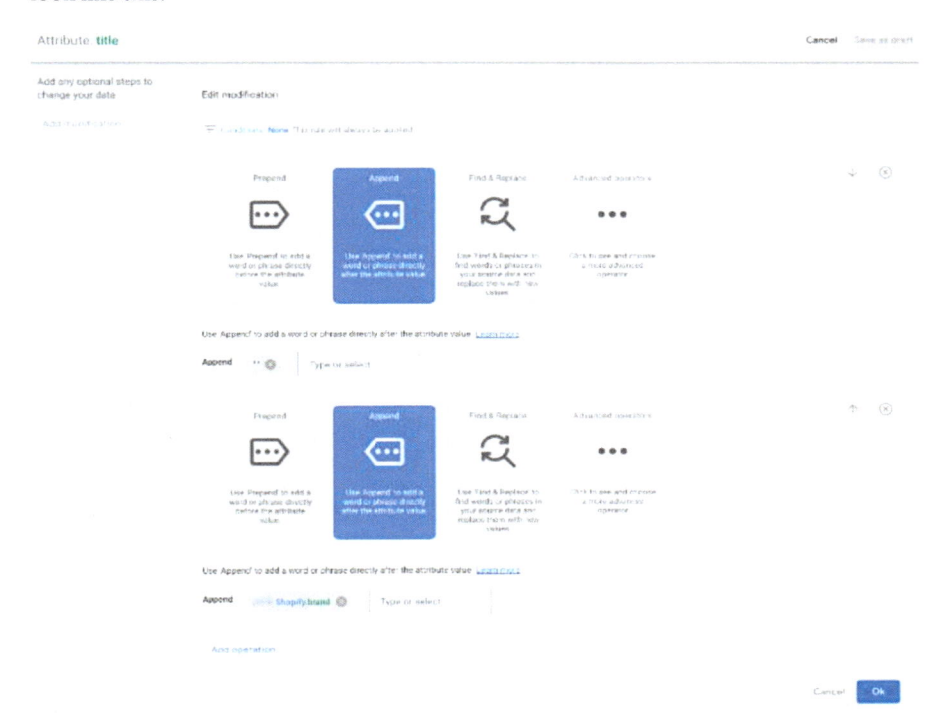

9. Click OK and then save the draft. Now you can celebrate your first rule!

Extract Material from Description

There will be times when products that are in the apparel category will be missing the material attribute. You can often find references to the materials that make up the product in the description. In this example. I will set up a rule to automatically extract the material from the description and apply it to the material attribute.

1. Click on the blue + button.

2. Find the source that you want to edit. In this case it will be "material" found under Processed attributes. This will open a new screen.

3. On the left-hand side you should see Data Sources—I will choose "Extract" for this example. Set the source to "Description."

4. In the "look for these words…" section I added:

Cotton

Rayon

Nylon

When the feed runs, the rule will look for each of these words and populate the material attribute if it finds one. Your rule should look something like the example below.

Note: You can see on the right side that for this product, it found cotton in the description, and it will populate the material attribute with "Cotton" if the attribute is empty.

5. Save as a draft and test your rule. Apply the rule if you are satisfied with the results.

Set the Promotion ID

There will come a time that you will want to set a promotion for a specific group of products. In this example I will set the promotion ID for hoodies.

1. Click on the blue + button.

2. Find the source that you want to edit which will be "promotion id" found under Processed attributes. This will open a new screen.

3. Click on "Set to" and fill in the value that you want for your promotion ID. This does not show to the customer. Use a name that is descriptive enough so you will remember it. Also, you cannot use the same ID more than once.

4. Click on conditions and choose product type. I added the value "hoodie," so when the product type has hoodie in it, the promotion ID will be updated.

5. Click OK and save it as a draft.

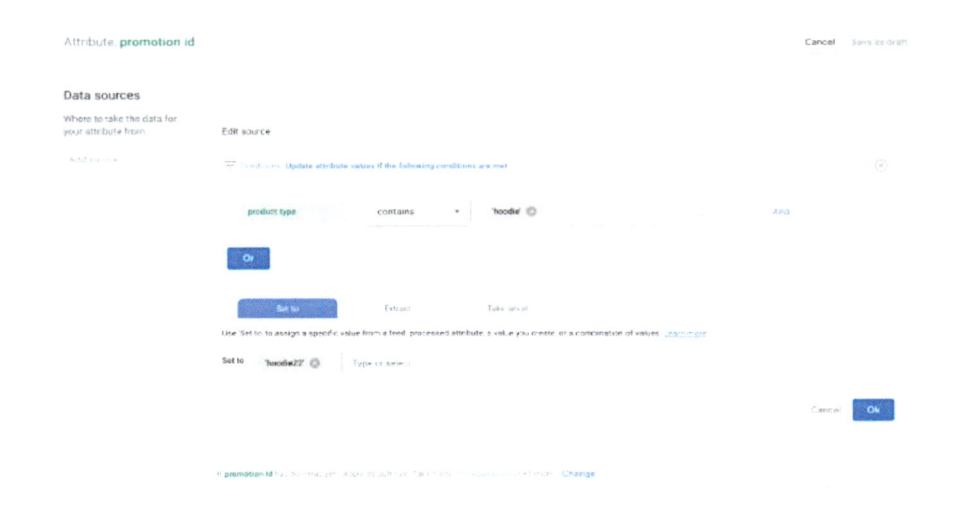

Summary

Feed rules are a powerful tool that can help you ensure that your product data is accurate and up to date. Feed rules can help you troubleshoot issues with your product data, and they can even help you improve your product listings in Google Shopping. If you are not using feed rules to manage your product data, you are missing out on a valuable opportunity to improve your product listings and keep your data accurate and up to date.

You can use feed rules to specify how your data should be formatted, what actions should be taken when certain conditions are met, and so on. The rules are processed in order, so you can use them to create a step-by-step workflow for your data. Feed rules provide a way for you to automate processing and can save you a lot of time and effort in managing your product data.

Chapter Thirteen

Parting Thoughts

It is no secret that Google is constantly changing the algorithms that govern how its search engine works. And while this can be frustrating for businesses who must continually adjust their SEO strategies, it ultimately benefits consumers by providing them with more relevant and useful search results.

However, as Google continues to make it easier and easier to get your products listed and advertised, the ability to stand out from the competition becomes more difficult. In such a crowded marketplace, it is essential to find ways to differentiate your business and make it more visible to potential customers.

Throughout the book, I have given you tips and best practices to set your listings apart from the competition. By taking the time to implement these strategies, you will be able to increase your visibility and attract more buyers.

So, what does the future hold? Google is constantly innovating to help businesses reach their target audiences. In the future, we can expect Google to continue to evolve, making it easier for businesses to connect with consumers and drive sales.

When I left Google, there was talk that in the future we would not need data feeds. This is a very real possibility, but as I have already outlined in the book, by the very nature of how a website is laid out, it is not conducive to clean product information.

It will take some time before websites are built in a way that Google can easily pull clean data. Until that time, the information I have provided here will help you optimize your feed and reach more customers. Most likely, there will always be a need for optimization, whether it is in the feed or in a feed portal like Google Merchant Center. The concepts I have covered here will continue to be applicable.

Google will continue to be a powerful player in eCommerce and product selling, and it will continue to innovate and make changes that will impact how we all do business. The best way to stay ahead of the curve is to keep tabs on their ever-changing policies and procedures and be nimble enough to adapt to the changes.

There are several resources to help keep you informed of Google's ever-changing landscape. I encourage you to sign up for the Google Shopping blog, as well as other eCommerce and online marketing blogs, to stay abreast of the latest changes.

In addition, Google offers free webinars and other educational resources to help businesses succeed. I encourage you to take advantage of these resources and stay up to date on the latest changes. I also am encouraging you to be wary. Google is a business that is trying to improve the bottom line. The latest and greatest might be wonderful for Google but not so good for you. Learn. Test. Evaluate.

In the first chapter, I stated that Google Shopping could level the playing field for your business if you optimize your feed. Before optimization, your feed is probably already equal to 50% - 60% of the retailers competing with you. Once you optimize, applying the tips and techniques outlined in the book, you will surpass 90% or more of your competition. That leaves you with just 10% to compete with on pricing and bid strategies. Not bad for something that, once it is set up correctly, will require very little management from a data perspective - making it a low-maintenance solution for success.

If you follow the advice in this book, you will be able to optimize your data feed quickly and easily, giving you a significant advantage over your competition. With just a few simple steps, you can make sure that your products are more visible and appealing to potential customers, leading to more sales and a healthier bottom line. So, what are you waiting for? Optimize your data feed now!

As the owner of a successful online marketing agency, I am frequently approached by businesses who are looking for help with their digital marketing efforts. Over the years, I have had the opportunity to work with businesses of all sizes, in a variety of industries. And while every business is unique, there are some common problems across the board. That is why I wrote this book—to share my knowledge and expertise with as many businesses as possible.

If you have found the information in this book helpful and are interested in learning more about how to grow your business online, I would be happy to provide additional resources and assistance. I offer a variety of consulting services designed to help businesses succeed in the digital age, and I would be happy to work with you to develop a customized plan that meets your specific needs. I am confident that I can help you take your business to the next level. Contact me today at kevinwetherby.com to learn more about my services and how I can help you grow your business online.

Acknowledgments

A big thank you to Eddie Roseboom for the cover design. His creativity and patience were much appreciated.

Thank you to John Gaset, for taking a chance and believing in a self-trained computer geek back in the day. He gave me a push down my tech path, and I will forever be grateful.

Thank you to my daughter Mickey for keeping my biggest fans, Mazie and Izzy, at bay while I was working (with promises of "fetch" and "keep away" later on.)

And finally, thank you to my wife Mary, whose persistence at perfection paid off in the end.

About the Author

Kevin J. Wetherby's journey to becoming a top revenue producer in online marketing started in the cabinetmaking business. His results-driven strategies crushed revenue goals for Fortune 500 companies, and he won multiple awards while working at Google on the Google Shopping team. When he isn't working, you'll find him surfing or fishing near Daytona Beach, Florida where life seems more perfect than ever before. Kevin loves to hear from his readers. Visit his website at www.kevinwetherby.com.